READ·WELL

Snapshots of the American West

Teacher's Guide

Unit 15

-or	-ment
•	•
means one who as in act<u>or</u>	as in apart<u>ment</u>

Note: See New and Important Objectives on page 2 for a complete list of skills taught and reviewed.

Critical Foundations in Primary Reading

Marilyn Sprick, Ann Watanabe, Karen Akiyama-Paik, and Shelley V. Jones

 Sopris West®
EDUCATIONAL SERVICES

A Cambium Learning® Company

BOSTON, MA • LONGMONT, CO

ISBN 13-digit: 978-1-60218-538-8
ISBN 10-digit: 1-60218-538-7

6 7 8 9 RRDHRBVA 14 13 12 11 10

166983/1-10

Table of Contents
Unit 15
Snapshots of the American West

End of the Unit

Letter Sounds and Combinations

Cumulative Review of *Read Well 1* Sounds and Combinations (Ss, Ee, ee, Mm, Aa, Dd, th, Nn, Tt, Ww, Ii, Th, Hh, Cc, Rr, ea, sh, Sh, Kk, -ck, oo, ar, wh, Wh, ĕ, -y as in fly, Ll, Oo, Bb, all, Gg, Ff, Uu, er, oo as in book, Yy, a schwa, Pp, ay, Vv, Qq, Jj, Xx, or, Zz, a_e, -y as in baby, i_e, ou, ow as in cow, ch, Ch, ai, igh, o_e, ir) and:

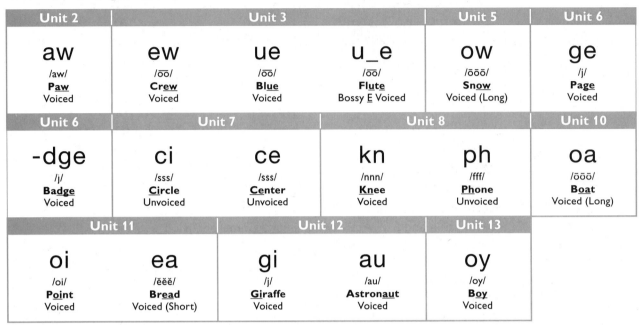

Affixes (including morphographs—affixes taught with meaning) and Open Syllables

Cumulative Review of *Read Well 1* Affixes (-ed, -en, -es, -ing, -ly, -s, -y, -tion) and:

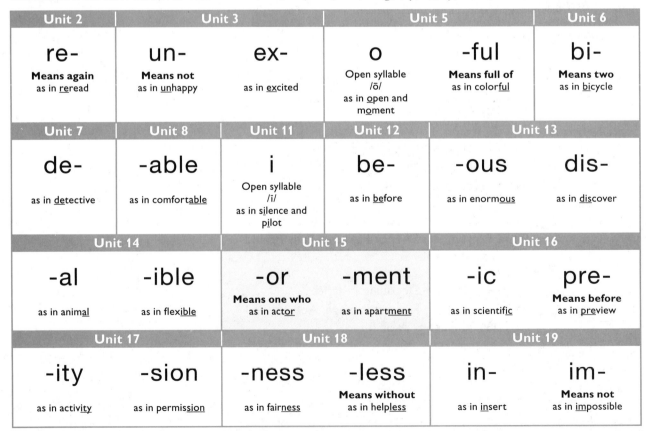

Introduction
Snapshots of the American West

Story Notes

Young America is the theme of Units 15 and 16. In these units, your students will continue building a sense of time and history.

Snapshots of the American West: The American West is the backdrop for fictional and nonfictional accounts of the United States in the 1800s. Students will read historical fiction—realistic accounts of hunting buffalos, building a sod house on the prairie, traveling along the Oregon Trail, and working on the transcontinental railroad. Nonfiction passages provide details about the importance of the buffalo to American Indian tribes, how tribes communicated, the hardships settlers faced as they moved to and settled in the West, and the impact of the transcontinental railroad.

Recommended Read Alouds

The *Read Well 2* suggested Read Alouds enhance small group instruction—providing opportunities to further build background knowledge and vocabulary.

The Girl Who Loved Wild Horses by Paul Goble
Fiction • Narrative
In this Caldecott Award–winning book, an American Indian girl develops a deep bond with the horses she tends. The connection between the girl and the horses becomes so strong that the girl eventually becomes one with the horses.

Apples to Oregon by Deborah Hopkinson
Fiction • Narrative
This hilarious story follows the journey of a pioneer family (and 700 fruit trees) along the Oregon Trail.

Read Well Connections
The Girl Who Loved Wild Horses complements Unit 15's fictional account of a young boy's first buffalo hunt. The entertaining story *Apples to Oregon* takes a lighthearted look at the challenges of traveling west in covered wagons.

> **CAUTION**
> **(Reminder)**
> Do not read the Read Aloud recommendations during small group instruction. Reserve this time for students to read.

NOTE FROM THE AUTHORS

> **YOUNG HISTORIANS**
> This unit gives your students the opportunity to learn more about time and history as they read passages and develop their own timeline. As they develop knowledge and an understanding of time and events in American history, congratulate your students on becoming young historians.

New and Important Objectives
A Research-Based Reading Program

Phonemic Awareness
Phonics
Fluency
Vocabulary
Comprehension

Phonological and Phonemic Awareness

Blending; Rhyming; Onset and Rime; Counting Syllables

Phonics

Cumulative Letter Sounds and Combinations

Review • Ss, Ee, ee, Mm, Aa, Dd, th, Nn, Tt, Ww, Ii, Th, Hh, Cc, Rr, ea, sh, Sh, Kk, -ck, oo, ar, wh, Wh, ĕ, -y (as in fly), Ll, Oo, Bb, all, Gg, Ff, Uu, er, oo (as in book), Yy, a (schwa), Pp, ay, Vv, Qq, Jj, Xx, or, Zz, a_e, -y (as in baby), i_e, ou, ow (as in cow), ch, Ch, ai, igh, o_e, ir, aw, ew, ue, u_e, ow (as in snow), ge, -dge, ci, ce, kn, ph, oa, oi, ea (as in bread), gi, au, oy

Cumulative Affixes, Morphographs, and Open Syllables

Review • -ed, -en, -er, -es, -est, -ing, -ly, -s, -y, -tion, re-, un-, ex-, o (as in open), -ful, bi-, de-, -able, i (as in silence), be-, dis-, -ous, -al, -ible

★New Letter Sounds, Combinations, Affixes, and Morphographs

-or (as in actor) • actor, collector

-ment (as in apartment) • agreement, government

★New Contractions

he'd

★New Proper Nouns

American Indian, American Indians, Arapaho, Browns, California, Cheyenne, Chinese, Gramps, Great Plains, Indiana, Indians, Irish, Irma, January, Kansas, Ma, Ming Mei, Mississippi River, Missouri, Montana, Nebraska, Oklahoma, Oregon, Pa, Rachel, Sierra Nevada, South Platte River, St. Louis, Swift Arrow, Ted, Utah, Willie

★New Pattern Words

ash, ashes, beef ◆ belts, boss, bosses, brace, brew, brews ◆ chunk, clothe, faint, flint, flour, grave, herd, ho, hoof, hooves, paste, phew ◆ pork, puff, puffy, raft, rafts ◆ rags, sauce, scout, scouts, self, selves, sledge, smoke, stove, thump, thumping, tribe, tribes, whipped

---

＊**Known Pattern Words With Affixes, Known Tricky Words With Affixes,** and **Known Multisyllabic Words With Affixes** have base words students have previously read. The words are new in this unit because they have not been previously read with the affix.

★ = New in this unit

◆ = Words that are not introduced in the exercises before they are read in the storybook

Phonics (continued)

*Known Pattern Words With Affixes • bends, blocked, bows, brains, brows, cheered, cooking, crossing, darkness, day's, drying, feelings, fewer, fired, folded, folks, grounded, grunts, joyously, knots, milked, nodding, pounded, rails, robes, rocking, rolling, sanded, sandy, scratching, slaves, snowing, sounded, spikes, streams, stuffing, tails, tents, traded, trades, unbends, unloaded, unloading

☆**New Compound and Hyphenated Words**

arrowheads, background, bowstrings, cradleboard, deerskin, dugout, farmhouse, firewood, floorboards, footsteps, gallstones, homestead, outdoors, railroad, railroads, sledgehammers
◆ snowman, steamboat, waterproof, windstorm

☆**Other New Multisyllabic Words**

◆ ahead, bacon, buffalo, buffalo's, bumpity, bumpy, candle, cedar, communicate, essay, former, legging, leggings, member, members, moccasins, muddy, oxen, paintings, pesky, photography, piano, pictographs, pioneer, pioneers, pony, pony's, powwows, purpose, rancher, ranchers, ravenous, reckon, reckons, regular, rely, reservation, reservations, scorcher, secret, settler, settler's, settlers, signals, tepee, uncle, willow

*Known Multisyllabic Words With Affixes • blankets, buckets, delivering, distances, gatherings, treasured

☆**New Tricky Words**

arrows, barrel, belief, beliefs, diary, fortune, meant, muscle, muscles, piece, prairie, prairies, sewing, soldier, soldiers

*Known Tricky Words With Affixes • created, journeyed, ties, tying, wolves

Fluency

Accuracy, Expression, Phrasing

Vocabulary

New • Arapaho, communicate, dangerous, distance, dugout, former, homestead, leggings, Missouri, pioneer, prairie, ravenous, rely, reservation, scorcher, scout, settler, the West, trade, trader, tribe, willow branch

Review • adventure, belongings, caption, community, curious, dawdle, destroy, dinosaur, embarrassed, exhausted, exhausting, fossil, frantic, immigrant, immigrate, impressed, ordinary, relative, roam

Reviewed in Context • adventure, allow, amazed, amazing, belongings, community, cram, custom, dawdle, embarrassed, except, exhausted, exhausting, expedition, generation, imagine, immigrant, perfect, pretend, survive, tradition, traditional, treasure, valuable

Idioms and Expressions

New • hold my head up high, make a name for ourselves

Comprehension

Unit Genres

Nonfiction • Expository

Fiction • Historical

Comprehension Processes

Build Knowledge: Factual, Procedural, Conceptual

Day	1	2	3	4	5	6
Remember						
Defining						
Identifying (recalling)	S,C	E,S,C	S	S	S,C	S,C
Using			S			S
Understand						
Defining (in your own words)	S	C	S	S,C	S,C	S
Describing	S		S	S	S	S
Explaining (rephrasing)	S	S	S	S		S
Illustrating						
Sequencing		E,C	C	C	C	
Summarizing	S,C	E,S	C		S	S
Using	S	S,C	S,C	S,C	S,C	S,C
Visualizing			S			
Apply						
Demonstrating	S	S	S			
Explaining (unstated)	S	S	S	S	C	S
Illustrating		C	C	C	C	
Inferring	S	S	S	S	S,C	S,C
Making Connections (relating)	S	S	S			S
Predicting	S		S		S	
Using	S	S	S	S	S	S
Analyze						
Classifying					S	
Comparing/Contrasting	S	S		S	S	S
Distinguishing Cause/Effect	C			S		S
Drawing Conclusions	S	S		S	S	C
Inferring						
Evaluate						
Making Judgments						
Responding (personal)	S		S	S	S,C	C
Create						
Generating Ideas		C	C	C	S,C	C

E = Exercise, S = Storybook, C = Comprehension & Skill

Comprehension (continued)

Skills and Strategies

Day	1	2	3	4	5	6
Priming Background Knowledge	S					
Setting a Purpose for Reading	S		S	S	S	
Answering Questions	S,C	S	S	S	S	S
Asking Questions						
Visualizing			S			
Comprehension Monitoring/Fix Ups						
Does it Make Sense?	C	C	C	C		
Looking Back						
Restating						
Summarizing						
Main Idea						
Retelling						
Supporting Details	S	S	C			S
Understanding Text Structure						
Title, Author, Illustrator	S	S	S	S	S	S
Fact or Fiction					S	
Genre (Classifying)	S		S	S	S	
Narrative						
Setting	S,C				S	
Main Character/Traits (Characterization)*	S			S*		
Goal						C
Problem/Solution						
Action/Events/Sequence	C				S	
Outcome/Conclusion						
Lesson/Author's Message						
Expository						
Subject/Topic		E,C			C	C
Heading						
Supporting Details (Facts/Information)	S	E,S,C	C	S		S,C
Main Idea	C					
Using Graphic Organizers						
Chart	C					
Diagram (labeling)						
Hierarchy (topic/detail)		C				C
K-W-L						
Map (locating, labeling)						
Matrix (compare/contrast)						
Sequence (linear, cycle, cause and effect)	S	E,C	S,C	S,C	S,C	S
Story Map						
Web						

E = Exercise, S = Storybook, C = Comprehension & Skill

* Narrator

Comprehension (continued)

Study Skills

Day	1	2	3	4	5	6
Alphabetical Order						
Following Directions						
Locating Information	S,C	S,C	C	S		
Note Taking						
Previewing	S					
Reviewing		S		S	S	S
Test Taking				C		C
Using Glossary			S	S	S	S
Using Table of Contents	S					
Viewing	S	C	C	C	C	S
Verifying						

Writing in Response to Reading

Day	1	2	3	4	5	6
Sentence Completion	C	C	C	C	C	C
Making Lists		C				
Sentence Writing		C	C	C	C	C
Story Retell/Summary						
Fact Summary			C			
Paragraph Writing						
Report Writing						
Open-Ended Response						C
Creative Writing			C			

Writing Traits

(Addressed within the context of Writing in Response to Reading)

Day	1	2	3	4	5	6
Ideas and Content						
Elaborating/Generating			C			
Organization						
Introduction						
Topic Sentence						
Supporting Details						
Sequencing						
Word Choice						
Sophisticated Words (Tier 2 and 3)			C			
Conventions						
Capital		C	C	C	C	C
Ending Punctuation	C	C	C	C	C	C
Other (commas, quotation marks)						
Presentation						
Handwriting			C			C
Neatness			C			C

E = Exercise, S = Storybook, C = Comprehension & Skill

Daily Lesson Planning

LESSON PLAN FORMAT

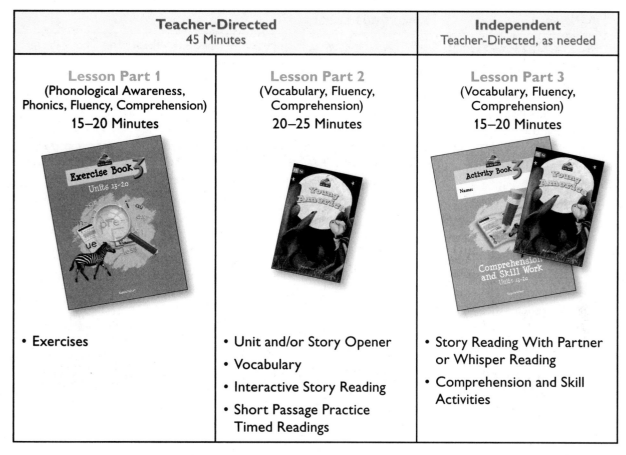

Teacher-Directed 45 Minutes		Independent Teacher-Directed, as needed
Lesson Part 1 (Phonological Awareness, Phonics, Fluency, Comprehension) 15–20 Minutes	**Lesson Part 2** (Vocabulary, Fluency, Comprehension) 20–25 Minutes	**Lesson Part 3** (Vocabulary, Fluency, Comprehension) 15–20 Minutes
• Exercises	• Unit and/or Story Opener • Vocabulary • Interactive Story Reading • Short Passage Practice Timed Readings	• Story Reading With Partner or Whisper Reading • Comprehension and Skill Activities

HOMEWORK

Read Well Homework (blackline masters of new *Read Well 2* passages) provides an opportunity for children to celebrate accomplishments with parents. Homework should be sent home on routine days.

ORAL READING FLUENCY ASSESSMENT

Upon completion of this unit, assess each student and proceed to Unit 16, as appropriate.

WRITTEN ASSESSMENT

During the time students would normally complete Comprehension and Skill Activities, students will be administered a Written Assessment that can be found on page 107 in the students' *Activity Book 3*.

Note: See Making Decisions for additional assessment information.

DIFFERENTIATED LESSON PLANS

The differentiated lesson plans illustrate how to use materials for students with various learning needs. As you set up your unit plan, always include *Read Well 2* Exercises and Story Reading on a daily basis. Unit 15 includes 6-, 8-, 9-, 10-, and 11-Day Plans.

Plans	For groups that:
6-DAY	Complete Oral Reading Fluency Assessments with Passes and Strong Passes
8-DAY	Complete Oral Reading Fluency Assessments with Passes and require teacher-guided assistance with Story Reading and Comprehension and Skill Work
9-, 10-, or 11-DAY	Have difficulty passing the unit Oral Reading Fluency Assessments

6-DAY PLAN

Day 1

Teacher-Directed
• Exercise 1
• Unit and Story Opener: Snapshots of the American West
• Vocabulary, Ch. 1, 2
• Snapshots of the American West, Introduction, Ch. 1
• Guide practice, as needed, on Comp & Skill 1, 2

Independent Work
• On Your Own: Partner or Whisper Read, Snapshots of the American West, Ch. 2
• Comp & Skill 1, 2

Homework
• Homework Passage 1

Day 2

Teacher-Directed
• Exercise 2a
• Exercise 2b: Focus Lesson
• Vocabulary, Ch. 3
• Snapshots of the American West, Ch. 3
• Guide practice, as needed, on Comp & Skill 3

Independent Work
• Repeated Reading: Partner or Whisper Read, Snapshots of the American West, Ch. 3
• Timeline 1835, Comp & Skill 3

Homework
• Homework Passage 2

Day 3

Teacher-Directed
• Exercise 3
• Vocabulary, Ch. 4, 5
• Snapshots of the American West, Ch. 4
• Guide practice, as needed, on Timeline 1843, 1850; Comp & Skill 4, 5

Independent Work
• On Your Own: Partner or Whisper Read, Snapshots of the American West, Ch. 5
• Timeline 1843, 1850; Comp & Skill 4, 5

Homework
• Homework Passage 3

Day 4

Teacher-Directed
• Exercise 4
• Vocabulary, Ch. 6, 7
• Snapshots of the American West, Ch. 6
• Guide practice, as needed, on Timeline 1863, 1869; Comp & Skill 6

Independent Work
• On Your Own: Partner or Whisper Read, Snapshots of the American West, Ch. 7
• Timeline 1863, 1869; Comp & Skill 6

Homework
• Homework Passage 4

Day 5

Teacher-Directed
• Exercise 5
• Vocabulary, Ch. 8, 9
• Snapshots of the American West, Ch. 8
• Guide practice, as needed, on Timeline 1885, 1886; Comp & Skill 7

Independent Work
• On Your Own: Partner or Whisper Read, Snapshots of the American West, Ch. 9
• Timeline 1885, 1886; Comp & Skill 7

Homework
• Homework Passage 5

Day 6

Teacher-Directed
• Exercise 6
• Vocabulary, Ch. 10
• Snapshots of the American West, Ch. 10

Independent Work
• Repeated Reading: Partner or Whisper Read, Snapshots of the American West, Ch. 10
• Written Assessment
• Oral Reading Fluency Assessment*

Homework
• Homework Passage 6

Note: Unit 15 features an extra Just for Fun Comp & Skill activity, located after Activity 7. This page can be used any time after Chapter 4.

* The Oral Reading Fluency Assessments are individually administered by the teacher while students are working on their Written Assessments.

8-DAY PLAN • *Pre-Intervention*

Day 1

Teacher-Directed
- Exercise 1
- Unit and Story Opener: Snapshots of the American West
- Vocabulary, Ch. 1, 2
- Snapshots of the American West, Introduction, Ch. 1
- Guide practice, as needed, on Comp & Skill 1

Independent Work
- Repeated Reading: Partner or Whisper Read, Snapshots of the American West, Intro, Ch. 1
- Comp & Skill 1

Homework
- Homework Passage 1

Day 2

Teacher-Directed
- Review Exercise 1
- Review Vocabulary, Ch. 1, 2
- Snapshots of the American West, Ch. 2
- Guide practice, as needed, on Comp & Skill 2

Independent Work
- Repeated Reading: Partner or Whisper Read, Snapshots of the American West, Ch. 2
- Comp & Skill 2

Homework
- Extra Practice Word Fluency A

Day 3

Teacher-Directed
- Exercise 2a
- Exercise 2b: Focus Lesson
- Vocabulary, Ch. 3
- Snapshots of the American West, Ch. 3
- Guide practice, as needed, on Comp & Skill 3

Independent Work
- Repeated Reading: Partner or Whisper Read, Snapshots of the American West, Ch. 3
- Timeline 1835, Comp & Skill 3

Homework
- Homework Passage 2

Day 4

Teacher-Directed
- Exercise 3
- Vocabulary, Ch. 4, 5
- Snapshots of the American West, Ch. 4
- Guide practice, as needed, on Timeline 1843, Comp & Skill 4

Independent Work
- On Your Own: Partner or Whisper Read, Snapshots of the American West, Ch. 5
- Timeline 1843, Comp & Skill 4

Homework
- Homework Passage 3

Day 5

Teacher-Directed
- Exercise 4
- Vocabulary, Ch. 6, 7
- Snapshots of the American West, Ch. 6
- Guide practice, as needed, on Timeline 1850, Comp & Skill 5

Independent Work
- Repeated Reading: Partner or Whisper Read, Snapshots of the American West, Ch. 6
- Timeline 1850; Comp & Skill 5

Homework
- Extra Practice Word Fluency B

Day 6

Teacher-Directed
- Review Exercise 4
- Review Vocabulary, Ch. 6, 7
- Snapshots of the American West, Ch. 7
- Guide practice, as needed, on Timeline 1863, 1869; Comp & Skill 6

Independent Work
- Repeated Reading: Partner or Whisper Read, Snapshots of the American West, Ch. 7
- Timeline 1863, 1869; Comp & Skill 6

Homework
- Homework Passage 4

Day 7

Teacher-Directed
- Exercise 5
- Vocabulary, Ch. 8, 9
- Snapshots of the American West, Ch. 8
- Guide practice, as needed, on Timeline 1885, 1886; Comp & Skill 7

Independent Work
- On Your Own: Partner or Whisper Read, Snapshots of the American West, Ch. 9
- Timeline 1885, 1886; Comp & Skill 7

Homework
- Homework Passage 5

Day 8

Teacher-Directed
- Exercise 6
- Vocabulary, Ch. 10
- Snapshots of the American West, Ch. 10

Independent Work
- Repeated Reading: Partner or Whisper Read, Snapshots of the American West, Ch. 10
- Written Assessment
- Oral Reading Fluency Assessment*

Homework
- Homework Passage 6

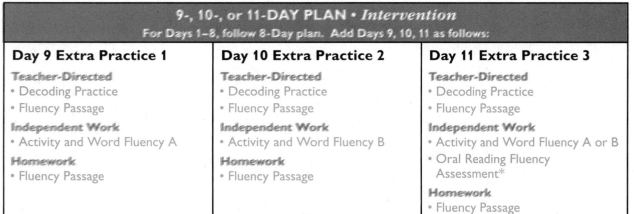

9-, 10-, or 11-DAY PLAN • *Intervention*
For Days 1–8, follow 8-Day plan. Add Days 9, 10, 11 as follows:

Day 9 Extra Practice 1

Teacher-Directed
- Decoding Practice
- Fluency Passage

Independent Work
- Activity and Word Fluency A

Homework
- Fluency Passage

Day 10 Extra Practice 2

Teacher-Directed
- Decoding Practice
- Fluency Passage

Independent Work
- Activity and Word Fluency B

Homework
- Fluency Passage

Day 11 Extra Practice 3

Teacher-Directed
- Decoding Practice
- Fluency Passage

Independent Work
- Activity and Word Fluency A or B
- Oral Reading Fluency Assessment*

Homework
- Fluency Passage

Materials and Materials Preparation

Core Lessons

Teacher Materials

READ WELL 2 MATERIALS

- Unit 15 Teacher's Guide
- Sound Cards
- Unit 15 Oral Reading Fluency Assessment found on page 116
- Group Assessment Record found in the *Assessment Manual*

SCHOOL SUPPLIES

Stopwatch or watch with a second hand

Student Materials

READ WELL 2 MATERIALS (for each student)

- *Young America* storybook
- *Exercise Book 3*
- *Activity Book 3* or copies of Unit 15 Comprehension and Skill Work
- Unit 15 Written Assessment found in *Activity Book 3*, page 107, and on the blackline master CD.
- Unit 15 Certificate of Achievement (BLM, page 117)
- Unit 15 Homework (blackline masters)
  See *Getting Started* for suggested homework routines.

SCHOOL SUPPLIES

Pencils, colors (optional—markers, crayons, or colored pencils)

> Make one copy per student of each blackline master, as appropriate for the group.
>
> *Note:* For new or difficult Comprehension and Skill Activities, make overhead transparencies from the blackline masters. Use the transparencies to demonstrate and guide practice.

Extra Practice Lessons

> **CAUTION**
> Use these lessons only if needed. Students who need Extra Practice may benefit from one, two, or three lessons.

Student Materials

READ WELL 2 MATERIALS (for each student, as needed)

See Extra Practice blackline masters located on the CD.

- Unit 15 Extra Practice 1: Decoding Practice, Fluency Passage, Word Fluency A, and Activity
- Unit 15 Extra Practice 2: Decoding Practice, Fluency Passage, Word Fluency B, and Activity
- Unit 15 Extra Practice 3: Decoding Practice, Fluency Passage, Word Fluency A or B, and Activity

SCHOOL SUPPLIES

Pencils, colors (optional—markers, crayons, or colored pencils), highlighters

> **SPECIAL NOTE**
> In this unit, your students will complete a timeline. For ease of use, pull pages 29–32 from *Activity Book 3*. Tape the pages down the center to create a folder.

> **FOCUS LESSON**
> For Exercise 2b (Focus Lesson), make overhead transparencies from the blackline masters, write on transparencies placed over the pages, or use paper copies to demonstrate how to complete the lessons.

Important Tips

Helping Low-Performing Students Comprehend

Some students require little instruction and guidance to understand and make inferences from what they read. Other students need ongoing instruction and practice to develop the knowledge, skills, and strategies that will eventually allow them to think deeply about what they read.

GUIDELINES FOR STORY READING

1. **Follow procedures.**

    When working with low-performing students, it is especially important to maintain program fidelity. Gray text questions in the storybooks and bird note discussion tips in the teacher's guides help students:
    *   build a cohesive understanding of the story.
    *   direct students' attention to information that will help them make inferences and draw conclusions.
    *   prepare students for written responses.

2. **Provide explicit teaching.**

    If students have difficulty comprehending during Story Reading:
    *   think aloud with them (model or demonstrate how you make an inference or draw a conclusion) and/or
    *   have them look back and reread the portion of the story that answers the question
    *   then repeat the question.

EXAMPLE, UNIT 15

Chapter 1, Buffalo Hunt

In Story Reading 1 of this unit, students read a narrative about two young Arapaho boys who go on a buffalo hunt. In this story, the setting—when and where the story took place—is central to understanding the story.

To help students understand how time affects events, students are introduced to a timeline. Throughout the unit, the timeline will be used to help students understand events and their relationship to history.

1. Timeline

Scaffold

Study the "Timeline" bird note. The script demonstrates how to introduce the timeline and how to direct students' attention to information about the story setting. This instruction provides a scaffold to students' written work.

2. Written Work

Guided Lesson

In a guided lesson preceding Activity 1, the teacher has low-performing students orally answer questions before they proceed to written responses. The following script demonstrates how to help students use the strategy of looking back and also guides students to make connections with the prior learning.

Everyone, look at Activity 1.
Read item 1. (Setting: When and where does the story take place.)
The first item asks "when" the story took place. Does anyone know?
(long ago)
Yes, this story took place long ago. The story also told us the year. Does anyone remember what year it was?
(It was 18 something.)

Direct students back to the timeline in the text. Say something like:

Think Aloud.

I can't remember the exact year either. How can we find the answer?

Prompt using the strategy of looking back.

(look back)

Go back to page 22. This chapter has something special that will help us find when the story took place. Everyone,

Guide making connections with previous learning.

where should we look to find the date? (the timeline)

Everyone, touch the timeline. Find the buffalo and the year this story took place. When did "Buffalo Hunt" take place? (1835)

Restate the question.

Excellent. When you answer "when" the story took place, what will you write? (1835)

"Long ago" would also be correct, but "1835" is a better answer because it gives us a better idea of when.

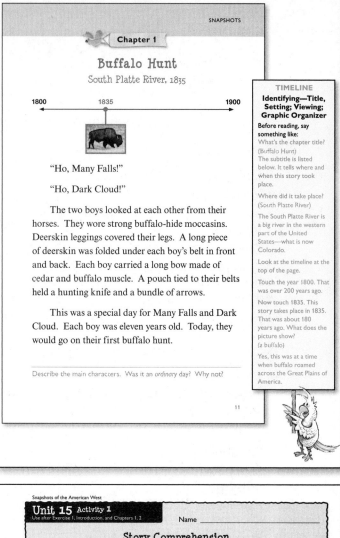

Chapter 1

SNAPSHOTS

Buffalo Hunt
South Platte River, 1835

1800   1835   1900

"Ho, Many Falls!"

"Ho, Dark Cloud!"

The two boys looked at each other from their horses. They wore strong buffalo-hide moccasins. Deerskin leggings covered their legs. A long piece of deerskin was folded under each boy's belt in front and back. Each boy carried a long bow made of cedar and buffalo muscle. A pouch tied to their belts held a hunting knife and a bundle of arrows.

This was a special day for Many Falls and Dark Cloud. Each boy was eleven years old. Today, they would go on their first buffalo hunt.

Describe the main characters. Was it an *ordinary* day? Why not?

11

TIMELINE

Identifying—Title, Setting; Viewing; Graphic Organizer

Before reading, say something like:
What's the chapter title? (Buffalo Hunt)
The subtitle is listed below. It tells where and when this story took place.

Where did it take place? (South Platte River)
The South Platte River is a big river in the western part of the United States—what is now Colorado.

Look at the timeline at the top of the page.

Touch the year 1800. That was over 200 years ago.

Now touch 1835. This story takes place in 1835. That was about 180 years ago. What does the picture show? (a buffalo)

Yes, this was at a time when buffalo roamed across the Great Plains of America.

Snapshots of the American West

Unit 15 Activity 1
Use after Exercise 1, Introduction, and Chapters 1, 2

Name _____

Story Comprehension
Buffalo Hunt

1. **Setting: When and where does the story take place?**
   When: 1835
   Where: South Platte River

2. **Initiating Event: Why was this a special day for Many Falls and Dark Cloud?**
   ○ The boys were eleven and going to have a birthday party.
   ● The boys were eleven and going on their first buffalo hunt.
   ○ The boys were going to learn to ride a horse.

3. **Action: What happened on the buffalo hunt?**
   You may wish to look in your storybook.
   1. The scouts led the men to a herd of ___buffalo.___
   2. The hunters yelled and rode fast. The herd started ___running.___
   3. The lead hunter drove one ___buffalo___ away from the rest.
   4. Many Falls and the other hunters fired their ___arrows.___

4. **Cause and Effect: How a main character got his name.**

Action		Outcome
• fell many times	→	• named ___Many Falls___

Action		Outcome
• quickly shot an arrow	→	• named ___Swift Arrow___

27

How to Teach the Lessons

Teach from this section. Each instructional component is outlined in an easy-to-teach format.

Exercise 1

- Unit and Story Opener: Snapshots of the American West
- Vocabulary
- Story Reading 1
  With the Teacher: Introduction, Chapter 1
  On Your Own: Chapter 2
- Comprehension and Skill Activities 1, 2

Exercise 2a

- Exercise 2b: Focus Lesson
- Vocabulary
- Story Reading 2
  With the Teacher: Chapter 3
- Timeline 1835, Comprehension and Skill Activity 3

Exercise 3

- Vocabulary
- Story Reading 3
  With the Teacher: Chapter 4
  On Your Own: Chapter 5
- Timeline 1843, 1850; Comprehension and Skill Activities 4, 5

Exercise 4

- Vocabulary
- Story Reading 4
  With the Teacher: Chapter 6
  On Your Own: Chapter 7
- Timeline 1863, 1869; Comprehension and Skill Activity 6

Exercise 5

- Vocabulary
- Story Reading 5
  With the Teacher: Chapter 8
  On Your Own: Chapter 9
- Timeline 1885, 1886; Comprehension and Skill Activity 7

Exercise 6

- Vocabulary
- Story Reading 6
  With the Teacher: Chapter 10
- Written Assessment

Note: Lessons include daily homework.

① SOUND REVIEW
Use selected Sound Cards from Units 1–14.

PACING
Exercise 1 should take
about 15 minutes.

② SHIFTY WORD BLENDING

③ ACCURACY AND FLUENCY BUILDING
C1. Compound Words
Have students tell you what a compound word is. Then have them read the words.
A compound word is made of two . . . (small words). Yes, a compound word is made of two small words. Read the compound words.

E1. Tricky Words
- For each Tricky Word, have students use the sounds and word parts they know to silently sound out the word. Use the word in a sentence to help with pronunciation.
- If the word is unfamiliar, tell students the word.

belief
Look at the first word. Say the word parts silently. Thumbs up when you know the word. Use my sentence to help you pronounce the word. Something that you think is true is a . . . *belief.* Read the word three times. (belief, belief, belief)

sewing
Say the word parts silently. Thumbs up when you know the word. Use my sentence to help you pronounce the word. My mom likes to make clothes. She enjoys . . . *sewing.* Read the word three times. (sewing, sewing, sewing)

piece
Sound the next word out silently. Thumbs up when you know the word. Use my sentence to help you pronounce the word. Mom cut the cake and gave us each one . . . *piece.* Read the word three times. (piece, piece, piece)

language   Do you speak more than one . . . *language?*
area   The sign said, "Please stay off the grassy . . . *area.*"

- Have students go back and read the whole words in the column.

④ WORD ENDINGS
Have students read each set of words.

⑤ MULTISYLLABIC WORDS
For each word, have students read the syllables, then the whole word. Use the word in a sentence, as appropriate. For Row C, have students read the whole words.

gallstones   Hard stones that can form in your gallbladder are . . . *gallstones.*
moccasins   Leather slippers that American Indians wore are called . . . *moccasins.*
Mississippi The big river that flows from Minnesota to the Gulf of Mexico is the . . . *Mississippi.*
pioneers   The people who settled in the West were . . . *pioneers.*
tepee   Gray Cloud's grandfather lived in a . . . *tepee.*
buffalo   Many American Indians hunted for . . . *buffalo.*

6 WORDS IN CONTEXT

For each word, have students use the sounds and word parts they know to silently sound out the word. Then have students read the sentence. Assist, as needed.

7 NAMES AND PLACES

Snapshots of the American West

Unit 15 Exercise 1
Use before the Introduction and Chapters 1 and 2

1. SOUND REVIEW Use selected Sound Cards from Units 1–14.

2. SHIFTY WORD BLENDING For each word, have students say the underlined part, sound out smoothly, then read the word.

dr<u>ank</u>	<u>th</u>ank	<u>bl</u>ank	<u>bl</u>ank<u>e</u>t	<u>bl</u>ank<u>e</u>ts

3. ACCURACY/FLUENCY BUILDING For each column, have students say any underlined part, then read each word. Next, have them read the column.

A1 Mixed Practice	B1 Mixed Practice	C1 Compound Words	D1 Word Endings	E1 Tricky Words
<u>h</u>erd	pesk<u>y</u>	insides	<u>tribes</u>	belief
knees	br<u>ai</u>ns	deerskin	<u>wagons</u>	sewing
thr<u>ea</u>d	p<u>ou</u>ch	photographs	<u>settlers</u>	piece
imagine	f<u>o</u>lded	bowstrings	<u>members</u>	language
bund<u>le</u>	sc<u>out</u>	railroads	<u>leggings</u>	area

4. WORD ENDINGS Have students read each word set.

dry	dried	fly	flies	hoof	hooves	knife	knives

5. MULTISYLLABIC WORDS Have students read each word part, then read each whole word.

A	gall•stones	gallsones	moc•ca•sins	moccasins
B	Mis•sis•sip•pi	Mississippi	pi•o•neers	pioneers
C	te•pee	tepee	buf•fa•lo	buffalo

6. WORDS IN CONTEXT Have students use the sounds and word parts they know to figure out each word. Then have them read each sentence.

A	mus•cles	The swift pony had powerful <u>muscles</u> for running.
B	ar•row	Uncle Ted uses a bow and <u>arrow</u> when he goes hunting.
C	ce•dar	Dad planted eleven <u>cedar</u> trees.

7. NAMES AND PLACES Have students use the sounds and word parts they know to figure out the words.

Great Plains	American Indian	Arapaho	Platte River

©2009 Sopris West Educational Services. All Rights Reserved.

COMPREHENSION PROCESSES
Remember, Understand, Apply

PROCEDURES

1. Introducing the Storybook

Identifying—Title; Priming Background Knowledge; Defining
Have students identify the title of their new storybook.
Say something like:

Everyone, look at the cover of your new storybook.
What's the title of your new storybook? (Young America)

That's right. Look at the picture.
The stories in this book took place in the 1800s in what is now the United States. That was about 100 to 200 years ago!
The Bone Wars took place in the 1800s.
What were the Bone Wars? (Two dinosaur hunters raced each other to find new dinosaur fossils.)

Like the Bone Wars, this unit is about things that happened long ago.
The stories are about events in the history of North America.

History is the study of things that happened in the past.
What do we learn about when we study history? (things that happened in the past)

2. Previewing the Unit

Using the Table of Contents; Identifying—Title, Genre; Predicting
Have students find the Table of Contents.
Say something like:
Everyone, find the Table of Contents.
What's the title of our new unit and story? (Snapshots of the American West)

Some of the chapters are nonfiction, and some of the stories are fiction.
What are fictional stories? (made-up stories . . .)
That's right. The fictional stories in this unit are also called *historical* fiction because the stories are made up, but they are based on real events that took place in the past.

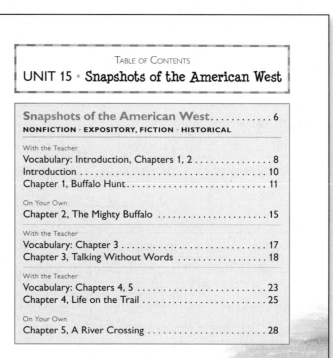

Look at the chapter titles. What are some of the things we'll read about? (a buffalo hunt, life on the trail, maybe cowboys or a wagon train . . .)

Let's turn to the title page for "Snapshots of the American West." What page does the story begin on? (page 10)

I'm looking forward to this unit. It's always interesting to learn how people long ago lived.

3. Introducing the Story

Using the Table of Contents; Identifying—Author; Making Connections

This story has 10 chapters. Each chapter was written by a different author. We're going to start with the introduction. Then we're going to read "Buffalo Hunt." Who is the author? (Bailey Phelps)

What other stories did Bailey Phelps write? (He wrote the legends "Centipede and Grandmother Spider" and "The War Between Birds and Mammals.")

The next story is a nonfiction story. Who are the authors? (Karen Akiyama-Paik and Shelley V. Jones)

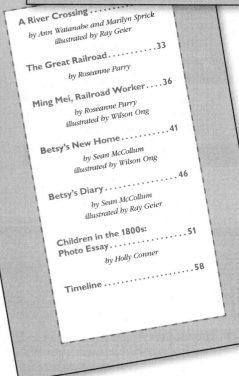

COMPREHENSION PROCESSES

Understand, Apply

PROCEDURES

Introducing Vocabulary

> ☆the West ☆pioneer
> ☆tribe ☆Arapaho ☆scout
> ☆leggings

- For each vocabulary word, have students read the word by parts, then read the whole word.
- Read the student-friendly explanations to students as they follow with their fingers. Then have students use the vocabulary word by following the gray text.
- Review and discuss the photos and illustrations.

USING VOCABULARY

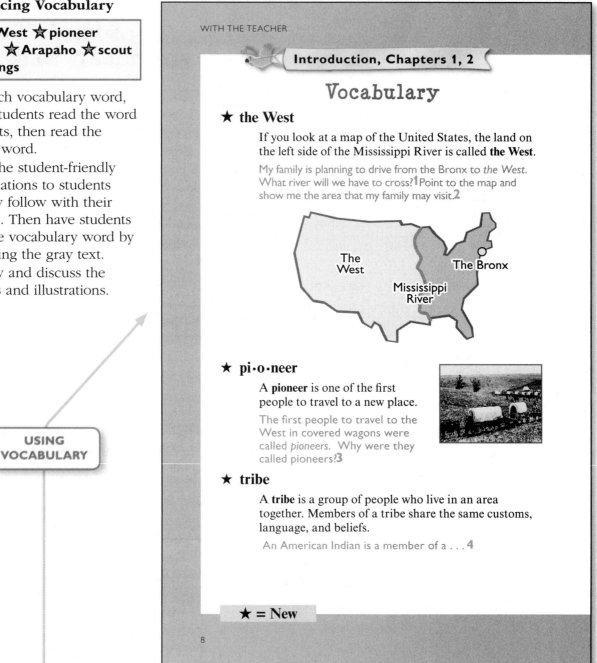

WITH THE TEACHER

Introduction, Chapters 1, 2

Vocabulary

★ **the West**

If you look at a map of the United States, the land on the left side of the Mississippi River is called **the West**.

My family is planning to drive from the Bronx to *the West*. What river will we have to cross?**1** Point to the map and show me the area that my family may visit.**2**

[map labels: The West, The Bronx, Mississippi River]

★ **pi·o·neer**

A **pioneer** is one of the first people to travel to a new place.

The first people to travel to the West in covered wagons were called *pioneers*. Why were they called pioneers?**3**

★ **tribe**

A **tribe** is a group of people who live in an area together. Members of a tribe share the same customs, language, and beliefs.

An American Indian is a member of a . . .**4**

★ = New

8

❶ **Apply:** Using Vocabulary—the West (You will have to cross the Mississippi River to get to the West.)

❷ **Apply:** Demonstrating; **Understand:** Using Vocabulary—the West

❸ **Understand:** Defining and Using Vocabulary—pioneer (Pioneers are the first people to travel to a new place.)

❹ **Understand:** Using Vocabulary—tribe (tribe)

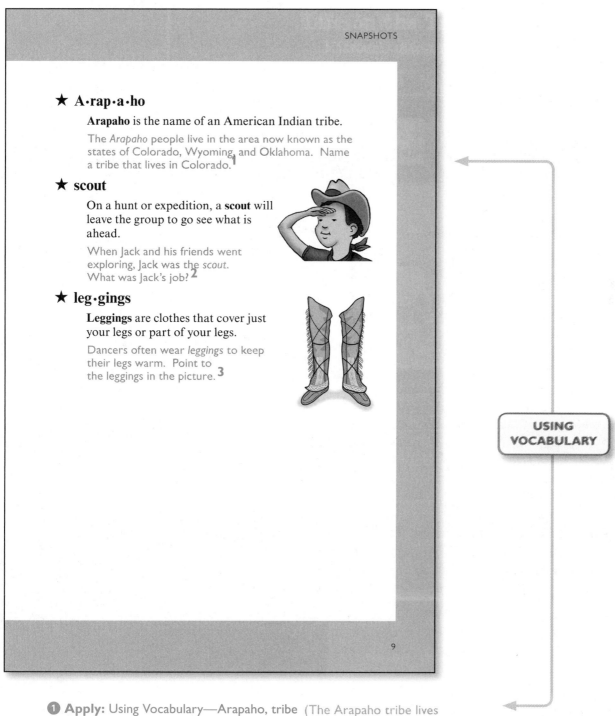

SNAPSHOTS

★ A·rap·a·ho

Arapaho is the name of an American Indian tribe.

The *Arapaho* people live in the area now known as the states of Colorado, Wyoming, and Oklahoma. Name a tribe that lives in Colorado.[1]

★ **scout**

On a hunt or expedition, a **scout** will leave the group to go see what is ahead.

When Jack and his friends went exploring, Jack was the *scout*. What was Jack's job?[2]

★ **leg·gings**

Leggings are clothes that cover just your legs or part of your legs.

Dancers often wear *leggings* to keep their legs warm. Point to the leggings in the picture.[3]

USING VOCABULARY

9

❶ **Apply:** Using Vocabulary—Arapaho, tribe (The Arapaho tribe lives in Colorado.)

❷ **Understand:** Defining and Vocabulary—scout (Jack's job was to go ahead of the group.)

❸ **Apply:** Demonstrating; **Understand:** Using Vocabulary—leggings

INTRODUCTION AND CHAPTER 1 INSTRUCTIONS

Students read the Introduction and Chapter 1 with the teacher and Chapter 2 on their own.

Note: If you're working on an 8- to 11-Day Plan, you will read Chapter 2 with students.

COMPREHENSION PROCESSES

Remember, Understand, Apply, Analyze, Evaluate

COMPREHENSION BUILDING

- Encourage students to answer questions with complete sentences, when appropriate.
- If students have difficulty comprehending, think aloud with them or reread the portion of the story that answers the question. Repeat the question.

PROCEDURES

1. Introducing the Introduction

Explaining

Say something like:

Turn to the Introduction on page 10.

Do you remember from our last unit what an introduction is?

(It tells you what the story is about.)

> **CORRECTING DECODING ERRORS**
>
> During story reading, gently correct any error, then have students reread the sentence.

2. First Reading

- Ask questions and discuss the text as indicated by the questions embedded in the text and by the gray text questions.
- Mix group and individual turns, independent of your voice.
  Have students work toward a group accuracy goal of 0–6 errors. Quietly keep track of errors made by all students in the group.
- After reading the story, practice any difficult words.
  Repeat, if students have not reached the accuracy goal.

3. Second Reading, Short Passage Practice: Developing Prosody

- Demonstrate expressive, fluent reading of the first paragraph. Read at a rate slightly faster than the students' rate. Say something like:

  Listen to my expression as I read the first paragraph.

  "Two hundred years ago, the West was a place where American Indian tribes lived as they had for hundreds of years. It was a place where pioneers traveled many miles to make new homes. What do you know about the American West in the 1800s?"

- Guide practice with your voice.

  Read the first page with me.

- Provide individual turns while others track with their fingers and whisper read.
- Repeat with one paragraph at a time.

> **REPEATED READINGS**
>
> **Prosody**
>
> On the second reading, students practice developing prosody—phrasing and expression. Research has shown that prosody is related to both fluency and comprehension.

WITH THE TEACHER

Introduction

Two hundred years ago, the West was a place where American Indian tribes lived as they had for hundreds of years. It was a place where pioneers traveled many miles to make new homes. What do you know about the American West in the 1800s?

Here are stories and photographs about the Old West—Indians, buffalo, pioneers, settlers, and the building of the railroads. Imagine that you lived in the Old West. What would your life have been like? Would you have hunted buffalo? Would your family have traveled west in a covered wagon? Would you have settled in a new home out West? Perhaps you would have helped build the railroads.

FOCUS ON COMPREHENSION

Contrasting, Responding, Making Connections

As students read the storybook, stop and discuss the questions embedded in the story.

What would your life have been like? (It would have been different. There would have been no TVs, no phones, no cars . . .)

Would you have hunted buffalo? (Yes, I think that would have been fun. No, I would not want to hunt animals.)

Would your family have traveled west in a covered wagon? (Yes, my dad likes adventure. No, my family would not want to move.)

10

SNAPSHOTS

Chapter 1

Buffalo Hunt

South Platte River, 1835

1800   1835   1900

"Ho, Many Falls!"

"Ho, Dark Cloud!"

The two boys looked at each other from their horses. They wore strong buffalo-hide moccasins. Deerskin leggings covered their legs. A long piece of deerskin was folded under each boy's belt in front and back. Each boy carried a long bow made of cedar and buffalo muscle. A pouch tied to their belts held a hunting knife and a bundle of arrows.

This was a special day for Many Falls and Dark Cloud. Each boy was eleven years old. Today, they would go on their first buffalo hunt.

Describe the main characters.**1** Was it an *ordinary* day? Why not?**2**

11

TIMELINE

Identifying—Title, Setting; Viewing; Graphic Organizer

Before reading, say something like:

What's the chapter title? (Buffalo Hunt)

The subtitle is listed below. It tells where and when this story took place.

Where did it take place? (South Platte River)

The South Platte River is a big river in the western part of the United States—what is now Colorado.

Look at the timeline at the top of the page.

Touch the year 1800. That was over 200 years ago.

Now touch 1835. This story takes place in 1835. That was about 180 years ago. What does the picture show? (a buffalo)

Yes, this was at a time when buffalo roamed across the Great Plains of America.

COMPREHENDING AS YOU GO

❶ **Understand:** Describing—Main Characters (Many Falls and Dark Cloud were American Indian boys. They were eleven years old. Each boy wore deerskin clothing and carried a long bow, arrows, and a hunting knife.)

❷ **Apply:** Inferring, Explaining; **Understand:** Using Vocabulary—ordinary (No, it wasn't an ordinary day. It was a special day—the boys' first buffalo hunt.)

WITH THE TEACHER

Like all Arapaho boys, Many Falls and Dark Cloud had learned to ride horses when they were very young. When Many Falls was only five, his father put him on a pony. He slipped off the pony's back and fell. Each time the boy fell, he tried again. This happened many times. The boy was given the name Many Falls. His uncle said, "Many Falls is very brave. When he falls, he is ready to try again."

Over time, Many Falls learned to ride well. He held onto the pony with his knees and used his legs and feet to tell his pony what to do. His hands were free to shoot his bow.

On the day of the big hunt, Many Falls and Dark Cloud followed the other hunters. The scouts saw a herd of buffalo. They led the men to the buffalo. The men would hunt for one buffalo, but only one.

What *tribe* did the boys belong to?[1] Do you think Many Falls' uncle is *impressed* with him? Why?[2]

12

COMPREHENDING
AS YOU GO

[1] **Apply:** Inferring; Explaining; Using Vocabulary—Arapaho, tribe (The boys belonged to the Arapaho tribe.)

[2] **Apply:** Inferring; Explaining; Using Vocabulary—impressed (Yes, Many Falls' uncle was impressed. He thought Many Falls was brave. When Many Falls fell off his pony, he would get up and try again.)

SNAPSHOTS

The hunters yelled and rode fast. The buffalo herd started running. The lead hunter was Red Knife. He rode his horse right beside the herd. He drove one buffalo away from the rest. It came straight at Many Falls!

Many Falls turned his horse and shot an arrow. The other men rode hard and fired arrows. When the hunt was done, Many Falls' uncle spoke to him.

"That was a swift arrow you shot," he said. "Tonight, we will tell the story of the hunt. From today, your name will be Swift Arrow." Swift Arrow was proud and very happy.

What was Many Falls' new name?**1** How did he earn his new name?**2**

13

COMPREHENDING
AS YOU GO

❶ **Remember:** Identifying—What (Many Falls' new name was Swift Arrow.)

❷ **Apply:** Inferring, Explaining (He earned his name by swiftly shooting an arrow at a buffalo during a hunt.)

Note: If needed, discuss the word "swift."

WITH THE TEACHER

Think and Talk

DRAWING CONCLUSIONS

1. How did the boy get the name Many Falls?

INFERENCE, EXPLANATION

2. Explain how Many Falls was able to shoot an arrow while riding a horse.

DRAWING CONCLUSIONS

3. Why do you think the men hunted for only one buffalo?

INFERENCE

4. Why did Many Falls' name get changed to Swift Arrow? Why was he happy and proud?

14

1 **Analyze:** Drawing Conclusions (He was given the name Many Falls because he kept falling off the pony he was learning to ride. He fell so many times he was named Many Falls.)

2 **Apply:** Inferring, Explaining (He held onto his horse with his knees and used his legs and feet to tell his horse what to do. His arrows were kept in a pouch tied to his belt. His hands were free to shoot an arrow.)

3 **Analyze:** Drawing Conclusions (They needed only one buffalo for food. American Indians hunted only for what they needed . . .)

4 **Apply:** Inferring, Explaining (Many Falls shot a swift arrow in the buffalo hunt, so he earned a new name. He was proud because his new name was better than his old name.)

CHAPTER 2 INSTRUCTIONS

Students read without the teacher, independently or with partners.

Note: If you're working on an 8- to 11-Day Plan, you will read Chapter 2 with students.

COMPREHENSION PROCESSES

Understand, Apply

PROCEDURES FOR READING ON YOUR OWN

1. Getting Ready

Have students turn to Chapter 2 on page 15.

Introduce the story by saying something like:

This next chapter is a nonfiction selection about American Indians and the buffalo. Is this a make-believe story? (no)

It is not make-believe. It is made up of . . . facts.

2. Setting a Purpose

Explaining—Facts

Before students begin reading, say something like:

Read to find out the answers to these questions:

- What parts of the buffalo did the Indians use?
- What were the different parts used for?

> **PREP NOTE**
> **Setting a Purpose**
> Write questions on a chalkboard, white board, or large piece of paper before working with your small group.

3. Reading on Your Own: Partner or Whisper Reading

- Have students take turns reading every other page with a partner or have students whisper read on their own.
- Continue having students track each word with their fingers.
- Have students ask themselves or their partners the gray text questions.

For Whisper Reading, say something like:

Everyone, turn to page 15. This is where you're going to start reading on your own—without me. Please whisper read with your finger, so I can see where you are in your work.

Turn to page 16. That's where you are going to stop reading.

For Partner Reading, say something like:

Everyone, turn to page 15. This is where you're going to start Partner Reading.

Where are you going to sit? (at our desks, side by side)

You will take turns reading pages. If you are the listener, what will you do?

(keep my book flat, follow with my finger, ask the gray text questions, compliment my partner)

If you are the reader, what will you do? (keep my book flat, finger track, read quietly, answer questions)

Turn to page 16. That's where you are going to stop reading.

4. Comprehension and Skill Work

For students on a 6-Day Plan, tell them they will do Comprehension and Skill Activities 1 and 2 after they read on their own. Guide practice, as needed. For teacher directions, see pages 29 and 30. (For 8- to 11-Day Plans, see the Lesson Planner, page 9.)

5. Homework 1: Repeated Reading

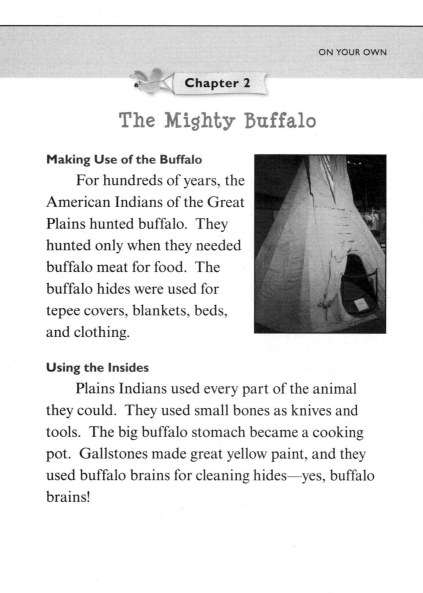

Chapter 2

The Mighty Buffalo

Making Use of the Buffalo

For hundreds of years, the American Indians of the Great Plains hunted buffalo. They hunted only when they needed buffalo meat for food. The buffalo hides were used for tepee covers, blankets, beds, and clothing.

Using the Insides

Plains Indians used every part of the animal they could. They used small bones as knives and tools. The big buffalo stomach became a cooking pot. Gallstones made great yellow paint, and they used buffalo brains for cleaning hides—yes, buffalo brains!

Why did the Plains Indians hunt the buffalo?[1] Look back at the last paragraph. Name four ways the American Indians used buffalo parts.[2]

15

COMPREHENDING
AS YOU GO

❶ **Understand:** Explaining (The Plains Indians hunted the buffalo for meat, for clothing, and to make tepees.)

❷ **Understand:** Locating Information; Summarizing—Facts (The Plains Indians used small bones as knives and tools. They used the stomach as a cooking pot. They used the gallstones as yellow paint, and they used the brains for cleaning hides.)

ON YOUR OWN

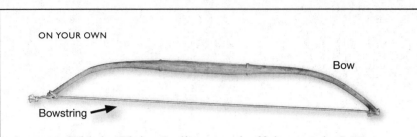

Bow

Bowstring ➜

　　　Did the Plains Indians use buffalo muscles? Yes, they dried buffalo muscles into bowstrings. They needed bowstrings on their bows so they could shoot their arrows while hunting. Indians also dried the muscles into sewing thread for making clothes.

Using the Outside

　　　What did they do with the hooves? Made glue! Did they use buffalo hair? Yes, they used the hair for rope and bed stuffing. What did they do with the horns? They drank from them. Last but not least, what about the buffalo's tail? Indians used buffalo tails in the same way the buffalo did—to shoo away pesky flies.

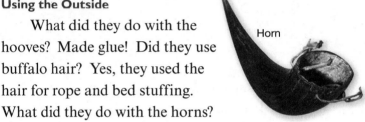

Horn

Tail

Name six more ways the Plains Indians used the buffalo.**1** Explain why the buffalo was so important to the Plains Indians.**2**

16

COMPREHENDING
AS YOU GO

❶ Understand: Locating Information; Summarizing—Facts (They used the buffalo muscles for bowstrings and thread. They used the hooves for glue. The hair was used for rope and bed stuffing. They also used the horns like cups. They even used the tail for a fly swatter.)

❷ Apply: Inferring, Explaining (The Plains Indians needed the buffalo for food and many other things like clothes, blankets, and tools. The buffalo was also important to the Plains Indians because they could use it in so many ways.)

STORY COMPREHENSION

COMPREHENSION PROCESSES

Understand, Apply, Analyze

WRITING TRAITS

Period

Identifying—Setting

Identifying—Initiating Event

Summarizing—Action

Distinguishing Cause/Effect

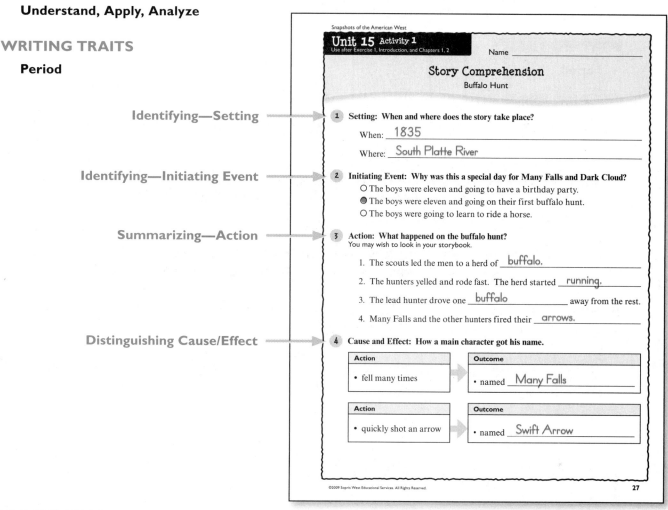

Snapshots of the American West

Unit 15 Activity 1
Use after Exercise 1, Introduction, and Chapters 1, 2

Name _____

Story Comprehension
Buffalo Hunt

1. **Setting: When and where does the story take place?**
   When: 1835
   Where: South Platte River

2. **Initiating Event: Why was this a special day for Many Falls and Dark Cloud?**
   ○ The boys were eleven and going to have a birthday party.
   ● The boys were eleven and going on their first buffalo hunt.
   ○ The boys were going to learn to ride a horse.

3. **Action: What happened on the buffalo hunt?**
   You may wish to look in your storybook.
   1. The scouts led the men to a herd of buffalo.
   2. The hunters yelled and rode fast. The herd started running.
   3. The lead hunter drove one buffalo away from the rest.
   4. Many Falls and the other hunters fired their arrows.

4. **Cause and Effect: How a main character got his name.**

Action		Outcome
• fell many times	→	• named Many Falls

Action		Outcome
• quickly shot an arrow	→	• named Swift Arrow

©2009 Sopris West Educational Services. All Rights Reserved.

27

PROCEDURES

For each step, demonstrate and guide practice, as needed. Then have students complete the page independently.

1. **Setting: Answering Questions—Basic Instructions** (Item 1)
   Have students fill in the blanks with the correct setting.

2. **Initiating Event: Selection Response—Basic Instructions** (Item 2)
   Have students read the question, then fill in the bubble with the correct answer.

3. **Action: Sentence Completion—Basic Instructions** (Item 3)
   Have students complete the sentences. Remind them to put a period at the end, where necessary.

4. **Cause and Effect: Answering Questions—Basic Instructions** (Item 4)
   Have students write the main character's name after each action.

Self-monitoring
Have students check and correct their work.

PASSAGE COMPREHENSION • MAIN IDEA

COMPREHENSION PROCESSES

Understand, Apply

WRITING TRAITS

Period

PROCEDURES

For each step, demonstrate and guide practice, as needed. Then have students complete the page independently.

1. **Chart: Answering Questions—Basic Instructions** (Item 1)
   - Have students read the headings on the chart and read the first row across.
   - Have students fill in the chart.

2. **Main Idea: Sentence Completion—Basic Instructions** (Item 2)
   Have students brainstorm what the main idea is, then complete the sentence.

Self-monitoring
Have students check and correct their work.

Using Graphic Organizer, Locating Information, Identifying—What

Identifying— Main Idea, Supporting Details

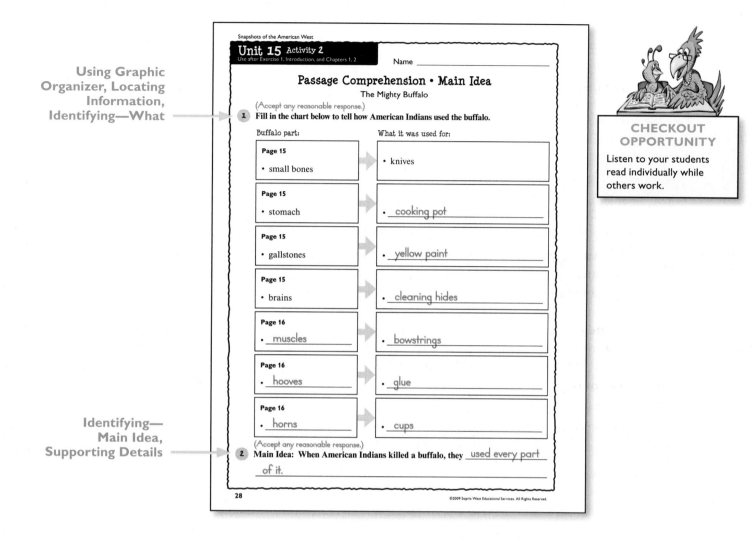

Snapshots of the American West

Unit 15 Activity 2
Use after Exercise 1, Introduction, and Chapters 1, 2

Name _____

Passage Comprehension • Main Idea
The Mighty Buffalo

(Accept any reasonable response.)

1 Fill in the chart below to tell how American Indians used the buffalo.

Buffalo part: What it was used for:

Page 15 • small bones	→	• knives
Page 15 • stomach	→	• _cooking pot_
Page 15 • gallstones	→	• _yellow paint_
Page 15 • brains	→	• _cleaning hides_
Page 16 • _muscles_	→	• _bowstrings_
Page 16 • _hooves_	→	• _glue_
Page 16 • _horns_	→	• _cups_

(Accept any reasonable response.)

2 **Main Idea: When American Indians killed a buffalo, they** _used every part of it._

28

CHECKOUT OPPORTUNITY

Listen to your students read individually while others work.

❶ SOUND REVIEW

Have students read the sounds and key word phrases. Work for accuracy, then fluency.

❷ SHIFTY WORD BLENDING

For each word, have students say the underlined sound, sound out the word, then say it.

❸ ACCURACY AND FLUENCY BUILDING

C1. Multisyllabic Words

- For the list of words divided by syllables, have students read each syllable, then the whole word. Use the word in a sentence, as appropriate.
- For the list of whole words, build accuracy and then fluency.

gatherings	Powwows are American Indian . . . *gatherings.*
distances	Long ago, immigrants walked great . . . *distances.*
powwows	American Indians gather together at . . . *powwows.*
communicate	People can use sign language to . . . *communicate.*
signals	When our teacher needs our attention, sometimes she raises her hand, claps in rhythm, or turns out the light. She uses . . . *signals.*

> **ACCURACY AND FLUENCY BUILDING**
> - For each task, have students say any underlined part, then read the word.
> - Set a pace. Then have students read the whole words in each task and column.
> - Provide repeated practice, building accuracy first, then fluency.

D1. Tricky Words

- For each Tricky Word, have students use the sounds and word parts they know to silently sound out the word. Use the word in a sentence to help with pronunciation.
- If the word is unfamiliar, tell students the word.

meant

Look at the first word. The word is *meant.* What Jake said is not what he . . . *meant.* Read the word three times. (meant, meant, meant)

warm	Colin's coat is nice and . . . *warm.*
ideas	Inventors come up with new . . . *ideas.*
sign	Turn right at the next stop . . . *sign.*

- Have students go back and read the whole words in the column.

❹ WORD ENDINGS

Have students read each word set. Tell students to note the spelling changes when the words have the endings added.

❺ MORPHOGRAPHS

- Remind students that a morphograph is a word part that means something.
- ★Introduce "or = one who."

  Look at Row A. The morphograph -*or* means one who. So we can say that *or*- equals one who. Everyone, read that with me. -or equals one who.

- For each word, have students read what the word means and the accompanying sentence. Have students rephrase the sentence.

  -*or* means one who, so actor means . . . one who acts. Read the sentence. (My father is an actor.) That means . . . My father is one who acts.

- Repeat with "creator equals one who creates."

★ = New in this unit

6 WORDS IN CONTEXT

For each word, have students use the sounds and word parts they know to silently sound out the word. Then have students read the sentence. Assist, as needed.

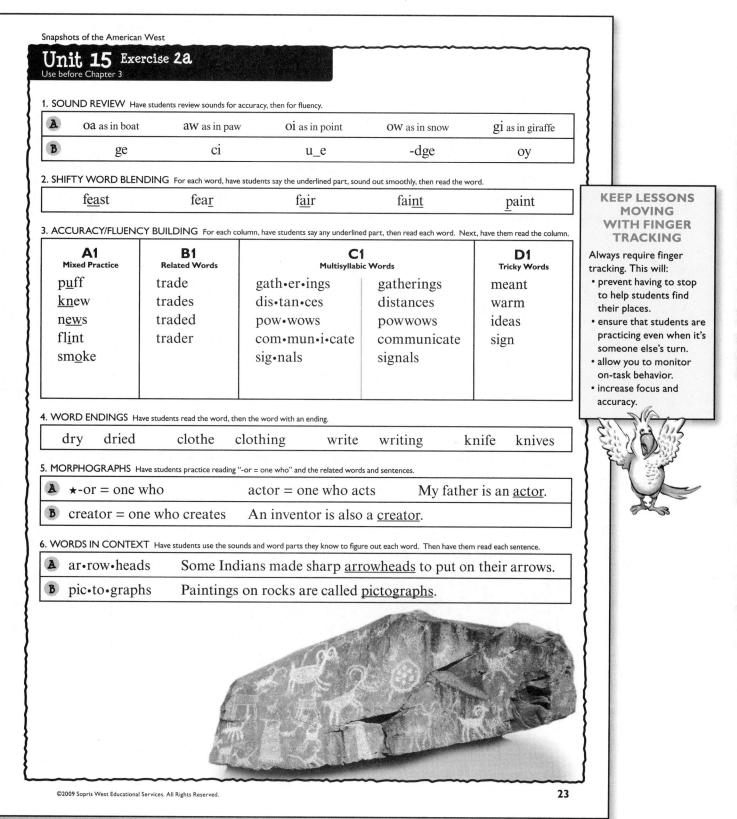

Snapshots of the American West

Unit 15 Exercise **2a**
Use before Chapter 3

1. SOUND REVIEW Have students review sounds for accuracy, then for fluency.

A	oa as in boat	aw as in paw	oi as in point	ow as in snow	gi as in giraffe
B	ge	ci	u_e	-dge	oy

2. SHIFTY WORD BLENDING For each word, have students say the underlined part, sound out smoothly, then read the word.

feast	fear	fair	faint	paint

3. ACCURACY/FLUENCY BUILDING For each column, have students say any underlined part, then read each word. Next, have them read the column.

A1 Mixed Practice	B1 Related Words	C1 Multisyllabic Words		D1 Tricky Words
puff	trade	gath•er•ings	gatherings	meant
knew	trades	dis•tan•ces	distances	warm
news	traded	pow•wows	powwows	ideas
flint	trader	com•mun•i•cate	communicate	sign
smoke		sig•nals	signals	

4. WORD ENDINGS Have students read the word, then the word with an ending.

dry	dried	clothe	clothing	write	writing	knife	knives

5. MORPHOGRAPHS Have students practice reading "-or = one who" and the related words and sentences.

A	★-or = one who	actor = one who acts	My father is an <u>actor</u>.
B	creator = one who creates	An inventor is also a <u>creator</u>.	

6. WORDS IN CONTEXT Have students use the sounds and word parts they know to figure out each word. Then have them read each sentence.

A	ar•row•heads	Some Indians made sharp <u>arrowheads</u> to put on their arrows.
B	pic•to•graphs	Paintings on rocks are called <u>pictographs</u>.

23

KEEP LESSONS MOVING WITH FINGER TRACKING

Always require finger tracking. This will:
- prevent having to stop to help students find their places.
- ensure that students are practicing even when it's someone else's turn.
- allow you to monitor on-task behavior.
- increase focus and accuracy.

TIMELINE

PURPOSE

This lesson provides explicit instruction in placing events on a timeline and writing a brief caption to summarize what was read. Across the unit, the related activities will help build students' understanding of time and cause and effect in history. The lesson also prepares students for Comprehension and Skill Work.

COMPREHENSION PROCESSES

Understand, Analyze

PROCEDURES

> **SPECIAL PREP NOTE**
>
> To demonstrate how to complete the exercise, use an overhead of page 24 in the students' *Exercise Book 3*, write on a transparency placed over the page, or use a paper copy.
>
> You may wish to complete a sample of the student timeline in Comp and Skill Work to show students what they will make in this unit.

① INTRODUCTION

Identifying—When

Introduce the timeline. Say something like:

In this unit, you're going to make your own timeline that shows events in American history—things that happened about 100 to 200 years ago. Look at the small timeline at the top of your Exercise. Touch the last dot.

It shows the year 2000. This is the year . . . ([2009]).

Touch the dot in the middle. What year does that show? (1900)

That was about 100 years ago. Touch the dot above the buffalo. What year does that show? (1800) That was about 200 years ago. Yesterday, we read an historical fiction story called "Buffalo Hunt." Find "Buffalo Hunt" on the gray timeline.

What year did it take place? (1835)

② WRITING A CAPTION

Identifying—Topic, Facts/Details; Using Graphic Organizer; Sequencing; Summarizing

Demonstrate and guide how to identify a topic and write a caption.

Now, we're going to write a caption about life during "Buffalo Hunt."

The caption will tell about the picture and about life during the time of the story.

What was the story about? (It was about a buffalo hunt.)

Who hunted buffalo? (American Indians) Yes, American Indians of the Great Plains hunted buffalo.

What did you learn from the story? (The boys got to hunt when they were eleven. They had special clothing. They earned their names . . .)

That information tells us a lot about buffalo hunts of long ago.

When we write our caption, we'll start with a topic. What could we start with?

(a buffalo hunt) Yes, we could also start with "American Indians" or "American Indian boys." Even better, we could start with "American Indians of the Great Plains."

Write "American Indians of the Great Plains" on your example.

Next, we need to write an important fact about American Indians and hunting buffalo. We could write, "American Indians of the Great Plains hunted buffalo for their food, tepees, and clothing." What else could we write?

(American Indians of the Great Plains taught their boys to hunt when they were about eleven. Some American Indians followed the buffalo.)

Those would all make great captions. I think I'll write "American Indians of the Great Plains were proud to hunt buffalo." **Write "were proud to hunt buffalo."**

Snapshots of the American West

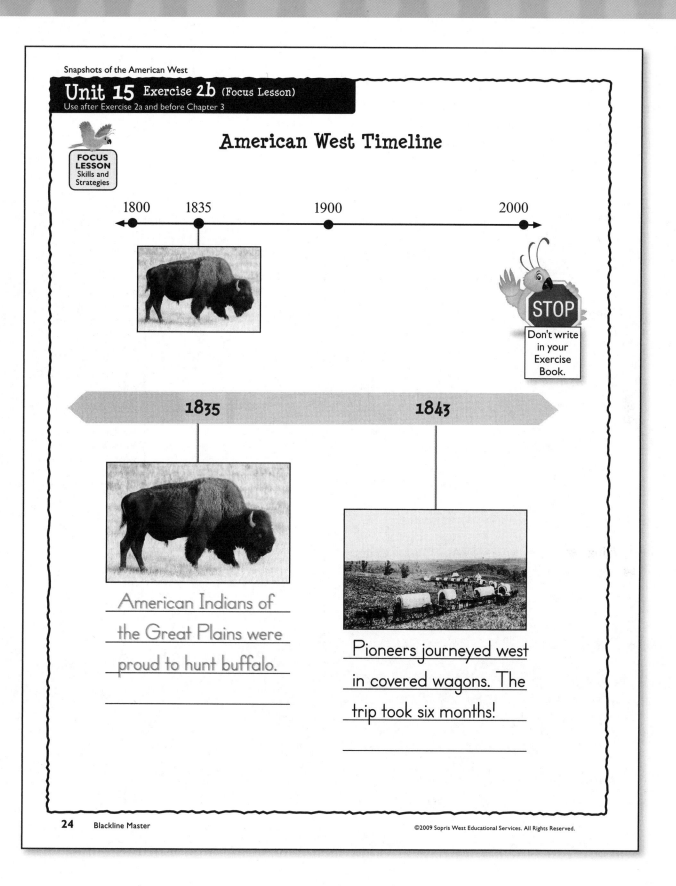

Unit 15 Exercise **2b** (Focus Lesson)
Use after Exercise 2a and before Chapter 3

FOCUS
LESSON
Skills and
Strategies

American West Timeline

1800   1835   1900   2000

STOP
Don't write
in your
Exercise
Book.

1835   1843

American Indians of
the Great Plains were
proud to hunt buffalo.

Pioneers journeyed west
in covered wagons. The
trip took six months!

24   Blackline Master

©2009 Sopris West Educational Services. All Rights Reserved.

35

COMPREHENSION PROCESSES
Understand, Apply

PROCEDURES
Introducing Vocabulary

> ☆ communicate ☆ trade ☆ trader ☆ distance

- For each vocabulary word, have students read the word by parts, then read the whole word.
- Read the student-friendly explanations to students as they follow with their fingers. Then have students use the vocabulary word by following the gray text.
- Review and discuss the photos and illustrations.

"The key to a successful vocabulary program is to use both formal and informal encounters so that attention to vocabulary is happening any time and all the time" (McKeown & Beck, p. 21, 2004).

Content Word Wall
Maintain a content word wall. Start with words from the storybook, then add to the list as students learn additional words related to the theme or topic. Encourage students to use the words in different contexts.

Note: Connections to other content areas will be easy to do because *Read Well* themes and topics are often related to classroom science and social studies instruction.

Students may wish to enhance the word wall by illustrating words with magazine pictures and drawings.

When *Read Well* instruction precedes classroom content-area instruction, the *Read Well* unit provides pre-teaching of vocabulary, inspires interest in a topic, and builds prior knowledge.

If science or social studies instruction follows a related *Read Well* unit, the *Read Well* unit provides review of vocabulary and content knowledge, and may extend content knowledge.

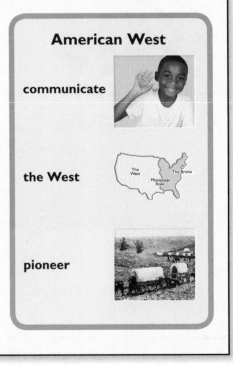

☆ = New in this unit

WITH THE TEACHER

Chapter 3

Vocabulary

★ **com·mu·ni·cate**

Communicate means to share ideas or feelings with someone else. You can communicate by talking, writing, making faces, or using your hands.

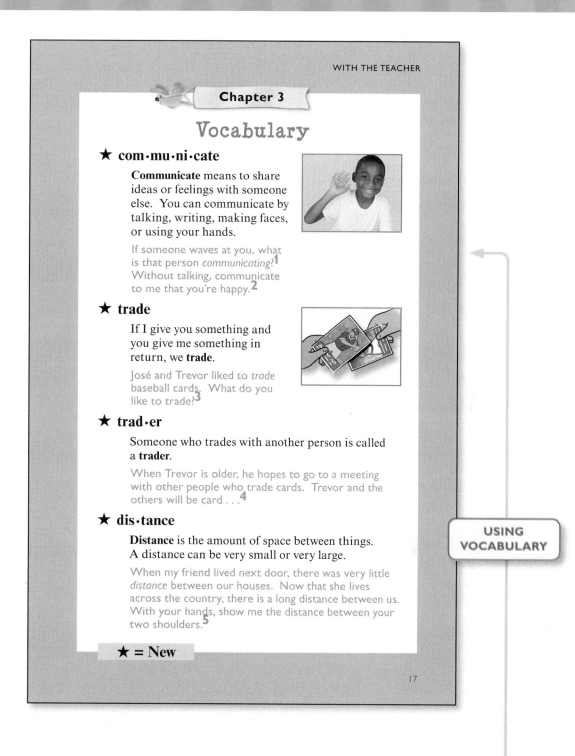

If someone waves at you, what is that person *communicating*?[1] Without talking, communicate to me that you're happy.[2]

★ **trade**

If I give you something and you give me something in return, we **trade**.

José and Trevor liked to *trade* baseball cards. What do you like to trade?[3]

★ **trad·er**

Someone who trades with another person is called a **trader**.

When Trevor is older, he hopes to go to a meeting with other people who trade cards. Trevor and the others will be card . . .[4]

★ **dis·tance**

Distance is the amount of space between things. A distance can be very small or very large.

When my friend lived next door, there was very little *distance* between our houses. Now that she lives across the country, there is a long distance between us. With your hands, show me the distance between your two shoulders.[5]

★ = New

17

USING VOCABULARY

① **Apply:** Using Vocabulary—communicate (If someone waves at you, he is communicating hello.)

② **Apply:** Demonstrating; Using Vocabulary—communicate

③ **Apply:** Making Connections; **Understand:** Using Vocabulary—trade (I like to trade comic books.)

④ **Understand:** Using Vocabulary—trader (traders)

⑤ **Apply:** Demonstrating; **Understand:** Using Vocabulary—distance

CHAPTER 3 INSTRUCTIONS
Students read Chapter 3 with the teacher.

COMPREHENSION PROCESSES
Remember, Understand, Apply, Analyze

PROCEDURES

1. Reviewing Chapter 2

Summarizing—Facts; Locating Information
Have students turn to page 15. Quickly discuss the questions from Chapter 2, Setting a Purpose. Say something like:

Yesterday, you read Chapter 2 on your own. Let's see what you found out.

There were a lot of facts, so you might want to look back in your book as we talk.

Turn to page 15 in your storybook.

What parts of the buffalo did the Indians use? (They used everything—hides, meat, muscles, brains, stomachs, gallstones, tails . . .)

What were the different parts used for? (The hides were used for tepees, clothing, and blankets. The muscles were used for bow strings. The brains were used for cleaning the hides . . .)

2. Introducing Chapter 3

Identifying—Title; Using Vocabulary—communicate
Read and discuss the title. Say something like:

What's the title of this chapter? (Talking Without Words)

What's your snazzy new word for talking, writing, and making faces? (communication)

Look at the title again. This story is about communicating . . . without words.

3. First Reading
- Ask questions and discuss the story as indicated by the gray text.
- Mix group and individual turns, independent of your voice.
  Have students work toward a group accuracy goal of 0–5 errors.
- After reading the story, practice any difficult words.
  Reread the story if students have not reached the accuracy goal.

4. Second Reading, Timed Readings: Repeated Reading
- As time allows, have students do Timed Readings while others follow along.
- Time individuals for 30 seconds and encourage each child to work for a personal best.
- Determine words correct per minute. Record student scores.

5. Partner or Whisper Reading: Repeated Reading
Before beginning independent work, have students finger track and partner or whisper read.

6. Comprehension and Skill Work
Tell students they will do Timeline 1835 and Comprehension and Skill Activity 3 after they read Chapter 3. Guide practice, as needed. For teacher directions, see pages 44 and 45.

7. Homework 2: Repeated Reading

WITH THE TEACHER

 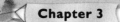

Chapter 3

Talking Without Words

More than 500 American Indian tribes live in North America today. At one time, the tribes spoke different languages (many still do), but they wanted to trade things with each other. This meant that they needed to talk with one another. They needed to communicate.

Talking With Sign Language

People from one tribe traded with others. One tribe might have warm buffalo robes and blankets. Another tribe might have a hard rock called flint. Flint is good for making knives, arrowheads, and other tools.

A trader with flint knives would meet another trader who had buffalo robes. The trader would put three knives on the ground. The other would shake his head "no." Three knives for a buffalo robe may not have been fair.

The first trader would try again. He would put down another knife. Then the second trader might have nodded "yes." Four knives for one robe may have been a good trade.

18

FOCUS ON VOCABULARY

Using Vocabulary— trade; Inferring

After reading the page, say something like:

In this example, the American Indians traded four knives for one buffalo robe.

Do you think that was a good trade? Why or why not?
(Yes, the robe would keep one trader warm, and the knives would be used for hunting, fishing, making things . . .)

Why didn't the Indians use money? (They didn't have money to trade with in the 1800s. They had the things they made.)

SNAPSHOTS

Nodding your head for "yes" or "no" is an example of sign language. You could also use your hands to sign. American Indians from many places learned to communicate in this way. They could talk about many things even though they did not speak the same language.

Why did the tribes *trade* with each other?**1** Why couldn't people from different tribes talk with one another?**2** Why was sign language important to American Indians?**3**

19

COMPREHENDING
AS YOU GO

❶ Apply: Inferring, Explaining; **Understand:** Using Vocabulary—tribe, trade (Each tribe had things that another tribe might need, so they traded.)

❷ Apply: Inferring, Explaining; **Understand:** Using Vocabulary—tribe (The tribes spoke different languages.)

❸ Apply: Inferring, Explaining; **Understand:** Using Vocabulary—communicate (They could communicate even though they spoke different languages. They could trade even though they spoke different languages.)

WITH THE TEACHER

Talking With Pictures

Another way to speak is with pictures. Some American Indians painted pictures on rocks. These are called pictographs. Some pictographs have survived for hundreds of years. The pictographs mark places that were special to a tribe. Pictographs are a way of saying, "Our people were here."

Talking With Smoke

Some tribes used smoke signals. This allowed people to communicate over long distances. Water or wet animal hide on a fire makes a puff of smoke. The smoke signals may have shared good news about a nearby buffalo herd.

Pictograph

Smoke Signal

Name two more ways American Indians sometimes communicated without talking. **1**

20

COMPREHENDING
AS YOU GO

1 **Understand:** Explaining—Facts; Using Vocabulary—communicate (American Indians sometimes communicated by painting pictures and using smoke signals.)

SNAPSHOTS

Powwows

Sometimes, thousands of American Indians from many tribes met in one place for many days. They traded dried meat, beads, clothing, tools, arrowheads, baskets, pots, and much more at these gatherings. People who knew more than one language would help others communicate.

Today, people from many tribes still meet at gatherings. These gatherings are called powwows. The people dance, sing, tell stories, and trade goods with one another.

Powwow 1800s   Powwow Today

What did American Indians trade in the past?**1** What is a powwow?**2**

21

COMPREHENDING
AS YOU GO

1 **Understand:** Explaining; Using Vocabulary—trade (American Indians traded dried meat, beads, clothing, tools, arrowheads, baskets, and pots.)

2 **Understand:** Explaining; Using Vocabulary—tribe, trade (A powwow is a gathering of American Indian tribes. People sing, dance, tell stories, and trade goods.)

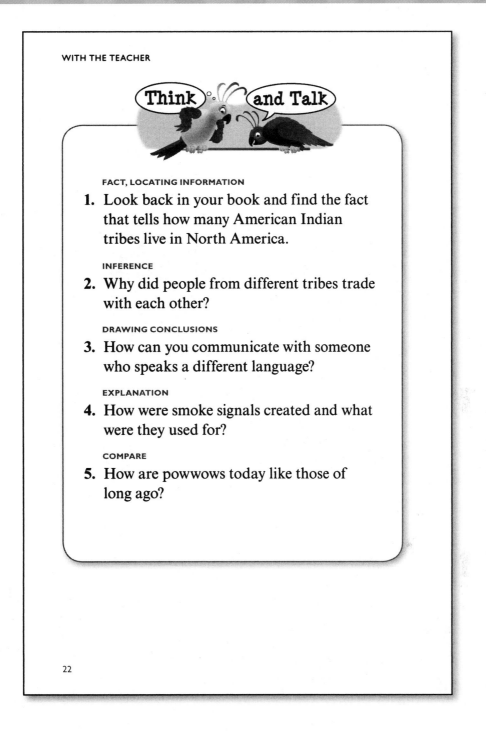

WITH THE TEACHER

Think **and Talk**

FACT, LOCATING INFORMATION

1. Look back in your book and find the fact that tells how many American Indian tribes live in North America.

INFERENCE

2. Why did people from different tribes trade with each other?

DRAWING CONCLUSIONS

3. How can you communicate with someone who speaks a different language?

EXPLANATION

4. How were smoke signals created and what were they used for?

COMPARE

5. How are powwows today like those of long ago?

22

❶ **Understand:** Locating Information; Identifying—Fact; Using Vocabulary—tribe (More than 500 American Indian tribes live in North America today.)

❷ **Apply:** Inferring, Explaining; **Understand:** Using Vocabulary—tribe, trade (Each tribe had things like blankets or flint that another tribe needed, so they traded.)

❸ **Analyze:** Drawing Conclusions; **Understand:** Using Vocabulary—communicate (You can communicate with sign language and pictures.)

❹ **Understand:** Explaining; Using Vocabulary—communicate, distance (First the Indians made a fire. Then they used water or wet animal hides to make a puff of smoke. The smoke signals were used to communicate over long distances.)

❺ **Analyze:** Comparing; **Understand:** Using Vocabulary—trade (Indian tribes of long ago gathered to trade goods. People still trade goods at powwows today.)

1835 • BUFFALO HUNT

COMPREHENSION PROCESSES
Understand, Apply, Analyze, Create

WRITING TRAITS
Conventions—Complete Sentence, Capital, Period

Using Graphic Organizer; Viewing Generating Ideas; Sentence Writing

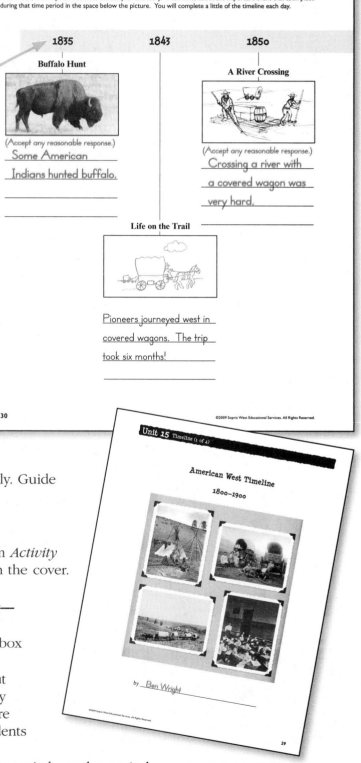

SPECIAL NOTE
Your students will complete a timeline. For ease of use, pull pages 29–32 from *Activity Book 3*. Tape the pages down the center to create a folder.

PROCEDURES
Have students complete the page independently. Guide practice, only as needed.

1. Preparation
After pages 29–32 have been removed from *Activity Book 3*, have students write their names on the cover.

2. Timeline: Sequencing, Caption Writing—Specific Instructions
- Have students look at the picture in the box under the date 1835.
- Have students write a short caption about "Buffalo Hunt." Remind students that they helped you write a caption for this picture during the Focus Lesson. Encourage students to write their own captions.
- Remind them to use a complete sentence, capitals, and a period.

PASSAGE COMPREHENSION • MAIN IDEA

COMPREHENSION PROCESSES
Understand, Apply

WRITING TRAITS

Defining and Using Vocabulary—
communicate

Using Graphic Organizer
Locating Information; Identifying—
Topic/Supporting Details

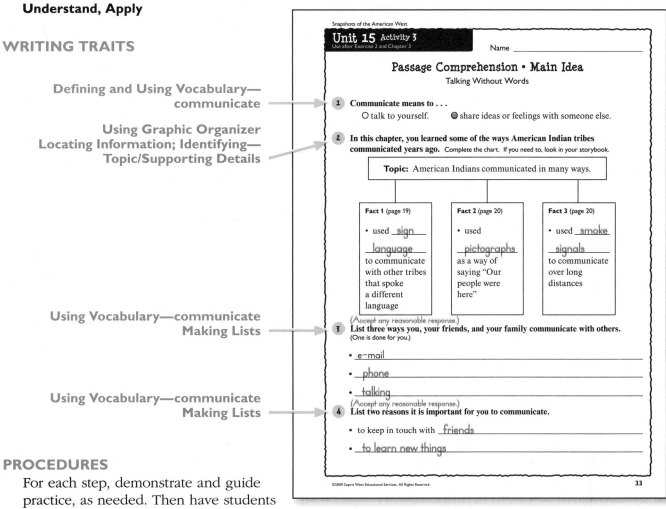

Snapshots of the American West

Unit 15 Activity 3
Use after Exercise 2 and Chapter 3

Name _____

Passage Comprehension • Main Idea
Talking Without Words

1 **Communicate means to . . .**
○ talk to yourself.　● share ideas or feelings with someone else.

2 **In this chapter, you learned some of the ways American Indian tribes communicated years ago.** Complete the chart. If you need to, look in your storybook.

Topic: American Indians communicated in many ways.

Fact 1 (page 19)	**Fact 2** (page 20)	**Fact 3** (page 20)
• used _sign_ _language_ to communicate with other tribes that spoke a different language	• used _pictographs_ as a way of saying "Our people were here"	• used _smoke_ _signals_ to communicate over long distances

(Accept any reasonable response.)

3 **List three ways you, your friends, and your family communicate with others.** (One is done for you.)

• e-mail
• _phone_
• _talking_

(Accept any reasonable response.)

4 **List two reasons it is important for you to communicate.**

• to keep in touch with _friends_
• _to learn new things_

©2009 Sopris West Educational Services. All Rights Reserved.　　33

Using Vocabulary—communicate
Making Lists

Using Vocabulary—communicate
Making Lists

PROCEDURES
For each step, demonstrate and guide practice, as needed. Then have students complete the page independently.

1. **Vocabulary: Selection Response—Basic Instructions** (Item 1)
   Have students read the sentence starter, then fill in the bubble with the correct definition.

2. **Topic/Supporting Detail: Hierarchy Chart, Sentence Completion—Specific Instructions** (Item 2)
   • Have students read the topic sentence.
   • Have students fill in the blanks to complete the supporting details.

3. **Vocabulary: Making Lists—Basic Instructions** (Item 3)
   Have students brainstorm ways to communicate with others, then list three.

4. **Vocabulary: Making Lists—Basic Instructions** (Item 4)
   Have students brainstorm why it is important to communicate with others, then list two reasons.

Self-monitoring
Have students check and correct their work.

① SOUND REVIEW
Use selected Sound Cards from Units 1–15.

② SOUND PRACTICE
- For each task, have students spell and say the focus sound in the gray bar. For Related Words, read the header.
- Next, have students read each underlined sound, the word, then the whole column.
- Repeat with each column, building accuracy first, then fluency.

③ ACCURACY AND FLUENCY BUILDING
- For each task, have students say any underlined part, then read the word.
- Set a pace. Then have students read the whole words in each task and column.
- Provide repeated practice, building accuracy first, then fluency.

C1. Shifty Words
For each word, have students say the underlined sound, sound out the word, then say it.

D1. Related Words
Tell students the words are related to the word *tie*. Then have them read the words.

E1. Names and Places
- Tell students these are people and places they will read about in the story.
- Have students use the sounds and word parts they know to figure out the words. Use the words in sentences, as needed.

④ MULTISYLLABIC WORDS
For each word, have students read the syllables, then the whole word. Use the word in a sentence, as appropriate.

difficult	The problem was not easy. It was . . . *difficult.*
waterproof	I can walk through the puddle because my boots are . . . *waterproof.*
continued	Sammy kept on talking. He . . . *continued* . . . to talk.
pioneers	The people who first settle in an area are called . . . *pioneers.*

⑤ MORPHOGRAPHS AND AFFIXES
- Have students read "-*or* equals one who" and the accompanying word and sentence.
- Then have students explain the sentence. Say something like:

  What does "The narrator tells the story" mean?
  (The one who narrates tells the story.)

- For row B, have students read the underlined part, then the word.
- Repeat practice with whole words, mixing group and individual turns.
  Build accuracy, then fluency.

⑥ GENERALIZATION: READING NEW WORDS IN PARAGRAPHS
- Have students read the paragraph silently, then out loud. Tell students to use the sounds and word parts they know to read any difficult words.
- Repeat practice, as needed.

Snapshots of the American West

Unit 15 Exercise 3
Use before Chapters 4 and 5

1. SOUND REVIEW Use selected Sound Cards from Units 1–15.

2. SOUND PRACTICE In each column, have students spell and say the sound, next say any underlined sound and the word, then read the column.

ea as in bread	-y as in baby	or	-le	Related Words
sw<u>ea</u>t	sand<u>y</u>	m<u>or</u>ning	catt<u>le</u>	bump
tr<u>ea</u>sured	And<u>y</u>	st<u>or</u>m	cand<u>le</u>	bump<u>y</u>
w<u>ea</u>ther	puff<u>y</u>	sc<u>or</u>cher	dawd<u>le</u>	bump<u>ity</u>

3. ACCURACY/FLUENCY BUILDING For each column, have students say any underlined part, then read each word. Next, have them read the column.

A1 Mixed Practice	B1 Word Endings	C1 Shifty Words	D1 Related Words	E1 Names & Places
o<u>x</u>en	<u>stream</u>s	<u>ph</u>ew	tie	Missouri
will<u>ow</u>	<u>ash</u>es	<u>br</u>ew	ties	Oregon
p<u>a</u>ste	<u>tent</u>s	brews	tied	Rachel
sw<u>a</u>m	<u>drip</u>ping	br<u>ow</u>s	tying	Pa
h<u>ar</u>sh	<u>dark</u>ness	Brow<u>n</u>s		Ma

4. MULTISYLLABIC WORDS Have students read each word part, then read each whole word.

(A)	dif·fi·cult	difficult	wa·ter·proof	waterproof
(B)	con·tin·ued	continued	pi·o·neers	pioneers

5. MORPHOGRAPHS AND AFFIXES Have students practice reading "-or = one who" and the related word and sentence. For row B, have students read each underlined part, then the word.

(A)	-or = one who	narrator = one who narrates	The <u>narrator</u> tells the story.
(B)	<u>un</u>bends	nerv<u>ous</u>	<u>ex</u>hausting	<u>be</u>longings

6. GENERALIZATION Have students read the paragraph silently, then out loud. (New words: raft, barrel, flour, reckons)

When Gramps was young, he went down the Mississippi river on a raft. He was delivering goods to folks. Suddenly a windstorm whipped up. His raft started rolling and rocking. Gramps was scared. A barrel of flour fell into the muddy river. He was afraid he might lose everything, but he got the raft to shore. Gramps reckons he was lucky to have survived.

25

BUILDING INDEPENDENCE
(Reminder)

Some students will try to follow your voice instead of learning to read the sounds and words. Therefore, it is important for you to demonstrate and guide practice only as needed.

Give students many opportunities to respond without your assistance—with groups and individuals. Encourage independence.

GENERALIZATION
(Reminder)

The generalization task provides an opportunity for you to informally assess students' ability to read new words that have not been pretaught.

COMPREHENSION PROCESSES

Remember, Understand, Apply

PROCEDURES

1. Introducing Vocabulary

> pioneer ☆ Missouri
> ☆ willow branch
> ☆ scorcher, exhausting,
> dawdle

- For each vocabulary word, have students read the word by parts, then read the whole word.
- Read the student-friendly explanations to students as they follow with their fingers. Then have students use the vocabulary word by following the gray text.
- Review and discuss the photos and illustrations.

USING
VOCABULARY

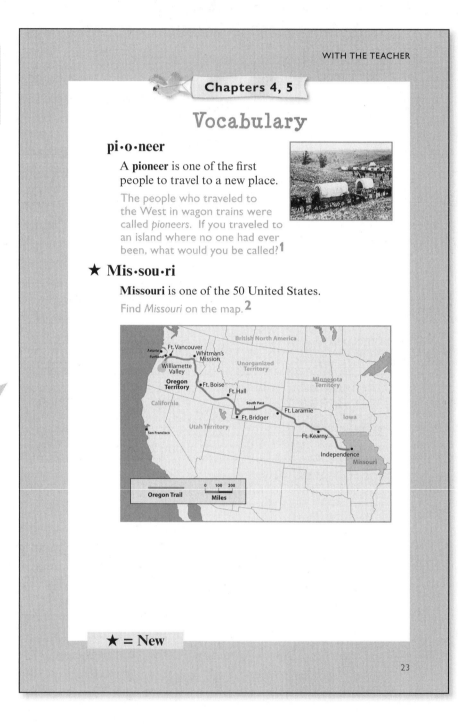

WITH THE TEACHER

Chapters 4, 5

Vocabulary

pi·o·neer

A **pioneer** is one of the first people to travel to a new place.

The people who traveled to the West in wagon trains were called *pioneers*. If you traveled to an island where no one had ever been, what would you be called?[1]

★ Mis·sou·ri

Missouri is one of the 50 United States.

Find *Missouri* on the map.[2]

★ = New

23

❶ **Understand:** Using Vocabulary—pioneer (I would be called a pioneer.)

❷ **Apply:** Demonstrating; **Understand:** Using Vocabulary—Missouri

☆ = New in this unit

2. Now You Try It!

- Read or paraphrase the directions.
- Then, for each word, have students read the word by parts, then read the whole word.
- Have students explain or define the word in their own words. Say something like:

  Look at the word. Say the parts, then read the whole word. (ex•haust•ing, exhausting) Now let's pretend that we're going to explain or define the word *exhausting* to a friend. [Jermaine], what would you say? Start with "*Exhausting* means . . . " (Exhausting means very tiring.) That's right. Exhausting means very tiring.

- Have students turn to the appropriate page in the glossary and discuss how their definitions are the same as or different from the glossary's. Your students may like their definitions better.

Note: By defining a word in their own words, students are demonstrating depth of word knowledge. Verbatim responses only demonstrate memorization. Encourage paraphrasing.

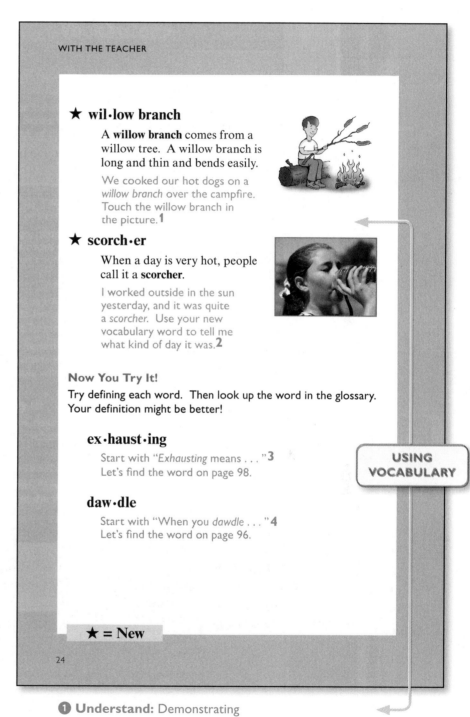

WITH THE TEACHER

★ **wil·low branch**

A **willow branch** comes from a willow tree. A willow branch is long and thin and bends easily.

We cooked our hot dogs on a *willow branch* over the campfire. Touch the willow branch in the picture. **1**

★ **scorch·er**

When a day is very hot, people call it a **scorcher**.

I worked outside in the sun yesterday, and it was quite a *scorcher*. Use your new vocabulary word to tell me what kind of day it was. **2**

Now You Try It!

Try defining each word. Then look up the word in the glossary. Your definition might be better!

ex·haust·ing

Start with "*Exhausting* means . . . " **3**
Let's find the word on page 98.

daw·dle

Start with "When you *dawdle* . . . " **4**
Let's find the word on page 96.

USING VOCABULARY

★ = New

24

❶ Understand: Demonstrating

❷ Understand: Using Vocabulary—scorcher
(Yesterday was a scorcher.)

❸ Understand: Defining and Using Vocabulary—exhausting; Using Glossary (Exhausting means very tiring.)

❹ Understand: Defining and Using Vocabulary—dawdle; Using Glossary (When you dawdle, you move slowly and take your time.)

CHAPTER 4 INSTRUCTIONS
Students read Chapter 4 with the teacher and Chapter 5 on their own.

COMPREHENSION PROCESSES
Understand, Apply, Evaluate

PROCEDURES

1. **Introducing Chapter 4**

   Identifying—Title; Predicting; Using Graphic Organizer—Sequence
   Say something like:

   Turn to page 25. What's the title of this chapter? (Life on the Trail)
   What do you think this chapter will be about?
   (It will be about wagon trains, going west . . .)
   When does this story take place? (Sometime between 1843 and 1869.)
   Look at the timeline. You read a story that took place in 1835.
   Which story was that? (Buffalo Hunt)
   What was happening in 1835? (American Indians were hunting the buffalo.)
   Why were the buffalo important to the American Indians?
   (The buffalo were used for food, tools, tepees, clothing . . .)

   "Life on the Trail" is a story that took place during this same time period.
   American Indians were hunting the buffalo, and pioneers were heading west to
   the same land.
   The year 1843 is just 8 years after the story about Many Falls.

2. **First Reading**
   • Ask questions and discuss the text as indicated by the gray text.
   • Mix group and individual turns, independent of your voice.
     Have students work toward a group accuracy goal of 0–3 errors.
     Quietly keep track of errors made by all students in the group.
   • After reading the story, practice any difficult words and reread,
     if appropriate.

3. **Second Reading, Short Passage Practice: Developing Prosody**
   • Demonstrate expressive, fluent reading of the first paragraph. Read at a
     rate slightly faster than the students' rate.
   • Guide practice with your voice.
   • Provide individual turns while others track with their fingers and
     whisper read.
   • Repeat with one paragraph at a time.

> **CORRECTING DECODING ERRORS**
> During story reading, gently correct any error, then have students reread the sentence.

SNAPSHOTS

Chapter 4

Life on the Trail

Missouri, 1843–1869

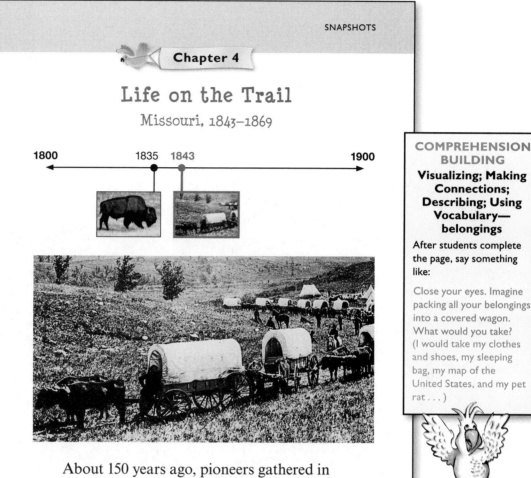

1800   1835   1843   1900

COMPREHENSION BUILDING

Visualizing; Making Connections; Describing; Using Vocabulary— belongings

After students complete the page, say something like:

Close your eyes. Imagine packing all your belongings into a covered wagon. What would you take? (I would take my clothes and shoes, my sleeping bag, my map of the United States, and my pet rat . . .)

About 150 years ago, pioneers gathered in Missouri to start a six-month journey west. Their wagons were crammed with their belongings and treasured things. Food was packed, and excitement filled the air.

By the end of the first day, pioneers had traveled about 15 miles. They had about 2,000 miles left to go.

25

Each day on the trail was full of adventure and hard work. If the weather was harsh, the day was difficult. If the trail was bad, the day was exhausting. Pioneers needed to cross the mountains by winter, or they would be blocked by snow. There was no time to dawdle.

26

Sometimes, the wagon trains had to cross a river. If a river was deep, the pioneers would lift their wagons off the wheels and float the wagons across the river.

Each morning by 4:00 a.m., with the sky as dark as night, pioneers were up and moving. They hurried in the darkness to make breakfast, milk the cows, round up the cattle, pull down tents, and load their wagons. Phew! By 7:00 a.m., the wagon train was rolling.

Bump, bump, bumpity, bump—the road was so bumpy that milk turned into butter by the evening.

Sometimes, a sudden windstorm whipped up the sandy dirt. By the end of the day, faces were covered with dirt and sweat. Eyes were red and puffy. Still, the pioneers got up the next day and continued on, trying to get to the West, where they could make new homes.

What made the trip west difficult? **1** Do you think you would have liked life on the trail? Why or why not? **2**

27

COMPREHENDING
AS YOU GO

❶ **Apply:** Inferring, Explaining; Using Vocabulary—pioneer (The trip west was difficult because the pioneers had to get up very early. The road was bumpy, and sometimes they would have to cross a river.)

❷ **Evaluate:** Responding; **Apply:** Explaining (I think it would have been fun, like camping every day. I would not have liked it because I like to sleep in my own bed. I don't like to get up in the dark. It sounds like it was a very long trip . . .)

CHAPTER 5 INSTRUCTIONS

Students read without the teacher, independently or with partners.

COMPREHENSION PROCESSES

Understand

PROCEDURES FOR READING ON YOUR OWN

1. Getting Ready

Have students turn to Chapter 5 on page 28.

2. Introducing the Chapter and Setting a Purpose

Identifying—Title, What, Genre; Explaining; Using Graphic Organizer; Inferring

Before students begin reading, say something like:

What's the title of Chapter 5? (A River Crossing)

This chapter is fiction. What does that mean? (It's a made-up story.)

Yes, and it is historical fiction. So what does that mean?

(The story is made up, but it is about real things that happened.)

Now look at the timeline. Touch the buffalo.

In what year did the "Buffalo Hunt" take place? (1835)

This story takes place during the years that pioneers headed west in covered wagons.

It takes place just 15 years after "Buffalo Hunt."

What year is this letter supposed to have been written? (1850)

That's a little more than 150 years ago.

This chapter is a letter from a boy to his grandfather.

Read to find out the answers to these questions:

- How did pioneers get wagons across a river?
- What happened to the Brown family?
- How do you think the pioneers felt when they got to a river?

> **PREP NOTE**
>
> **Setting a Purpose**
>
> Write questions on a chalkboard, white board, or large piece of paper before working with your small group.

3. Reading on Your Own: Partner or Whisper Reading

- Have students take turns reading every other page with a partner or have students whisper read on their own.
- Continue having students track each word with their fingers.

4. Comprehension and Skill Work

For students on a 6-Day Plan, tell them they will do Timeline: 1843 and 1850 and Comprehension and Skill Activities 4 and 5 after they read on their own. Guide practice, as needed. For teacher directions, see pages 58–61. (For 8- to 11-Day Plans, see the Lesson Planner, page 9.)

5. Homework 3: Repeated Reading

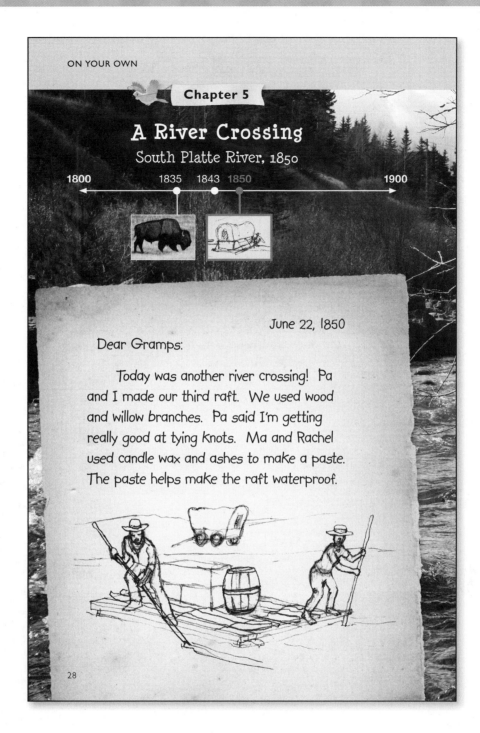

Chapter 5

A River Crossing
South Platte River, 1850

1800   1835   1843   1850   1900

June 22, 1850

Dear Gramps:

Today was another river crossing! Pa and I made our third raft. We used wood and willow branches. Pa said I'm getting really good at tying knots. Ma and Rachel used candle wax and ashes to make a paste. The paste helps make the raft waterproof.

28

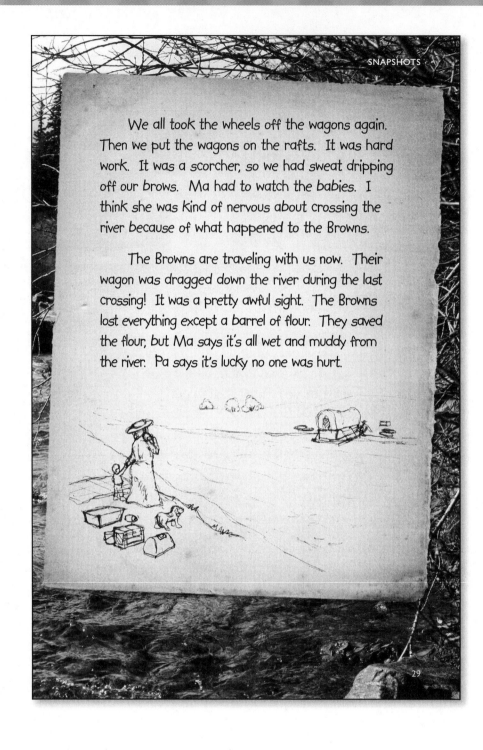

We all took the wheels off the wagons again. Then we put the wagons on the rafts. It was hard work. It was a scorcher, so we had sweat dripping off our brows. Ma had to watch the babies. I think she was kind of nervous about crossing the river because of what happened to the Browns.

The Browns are traveling with us now. Their wagon was dragged down the river during the last crossing! It was a pretty awful sight. The Browns lost everything except a barrel of flour. They saved the flour, but Ma says it's all wet and muddy from the river. Pa says it's lucky no one was hurt.

The river was calm today, so we got across this river just fine. Our oxen and horses swam to the other side. We didn't lose anything. Everything stayed tied down on the wagon. All the wagons are safe across the river. It was a good day.

Everyone says Oregon is a great place. They say there are tall trees and rivers and streams filled with fish. Pa says the land is good for farming. We reckon it will be a long time before we get there.

We miss you, Gramps. Hope this gets to you.
Love,
Andy

1843 • LIFE ON THE TRAIL AND 1850 • A RIVER CROSSING

COMPREHENSION PROCESSES

Understand, Apply, Analyze, Create

WRITING TRAITS

Conventions—Complete Sentence, Capital, Period

Using Graphic Organizer
Viewing; Illustrating; Generating Ideas
Sentence Writing

Unit 15 Timeline (2 of 4)

In each box, draw a picture to illustrate the year and story. Then write about the important event that took place during that time period in the space below the picture. You will complete a little of the timeline each day.

1835	1843	1850

Buffalo Hunt

(Accept any reasonable response.)
Some American
Indians hunted buffalo.

A River Crossing

(Accept any reasonable response.)
Crossing a river with
a covered wagon was
very hard.

Life on the Trail

Pioneers journeyed west in
covered wagons. The trip
took six months!

30

PROCEDURES

Have students complete the page independently. Guide practice, only as needed.

Timeline: Sequencing, Caption Writing—Specific Instructions
- Have students read the caption for 1843, "Life on the Trail."
- Have students draw a picture that illustrates the caption.
- Have students look at the picture under 1850 and write a short caption about "A River Crossing."
- Remind them to use a complete sentence, capitals, and a period.

PASSAGE READING

FLUENCY

Accuracy, Expression

PROCEDURES

For each step, demonstrate and guide practice, as needed. Then have students complete the page independently.

Passage Reading—Basic Instructions

• Have students read the practice words.

• Have students finger track and whisper read the story two times—the first time for accuracy and the second time for expression. Have students cross out a covered wagon each time they finish.

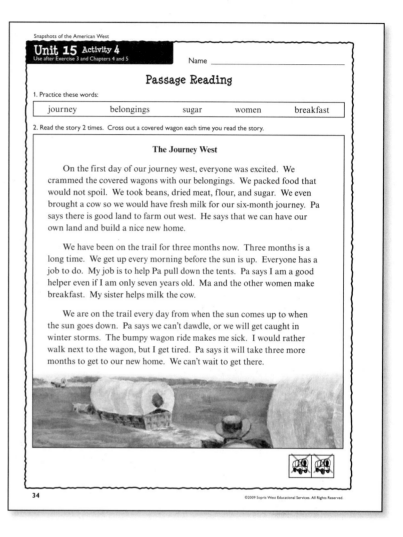

Snapshots of the American West

Unit 15 Activity 4
Use after Exercise 3 and Chapters 4 and 5

Name _____

Passage Reading

1. Practice these words:

| journey | belongings | sugar | women | breakfast |

2. Read the story 2 times. Cross out a covered wagon each time you read the story.

The Journey West

On the first day of our journey west, everyone was excited. We crammed the covered wagons with our belongings. We packed food that would not spoil. We took beans, dried meat, flour, and sugar. We even brought a cow so we would have fresh milk for our six-month journey. Pa says there is good land to farm out west. He says that we can have our own land and build a nice new home.

We have been on the trail for three months now. Three months is a long time. We get up every morning before the sun is up. Everyone has a job to do. My job is to help Pa pull down the tents. Pa says I am a good helper even if I am only seven years old. Ma and the other women make breakfast. My sister helps milk the cow.

We are on the trail every day from when the sun comes up to when the sun goes down. Pa says we can't dawdle, or we will get caught in winter storms. The bumpy wagon ride makes me sick. I would rather walk next to the wagon, but I get tired. Pa says it will take three more months to get to our new home. We can't wait to get there.

34

LOCATING INFORMATION • LETTER WRITING

COMPREHENSION PROCESSES

Understand, Apply, Create

WRITING TRAITS

Ideas and Content
Word Choice
Conventions—Complete Sentence, Capital, Period
Presentation

PROCEDURES

For each step, demonstrate and guide practice, as needed. Then have students complete the page independently.

1. **Fact Summary: Locating Information—Specific Instructions** (Item 1)
   Have students read the directions, then write things they learned about traveling west in a covered wagon. They can use information learned from Activity 4 or from their storybook.

2. **Letter Writing—Specific Instructions** (Item 2)
   Have students write a letter using the facts they listed in Item 1.

Self-monitoring
Have students check and correct their work.

**Locating Information
Summarizing—Facts**

**Generating Ideas
Creative Writing
Sentence Writing
Using—Facts**

Snapshots of the American West

Unit 15 Activity 5
Use after Exercise 3 and Chapters 4 and 5

Name _____

Locating Information • Letter Writing

(Accept any reasonable response.)

1 The passage from Activity 4, "The Journey West," is historical fiction. That means that even though the story is not true, it is based on facts. List three things about making the journey west in the 1800s. (The first one is done for you.)

• covered wagons packed with belongings

• everyone has a job

• bumpy ride, makes kid sick

(Accept any reasonable response.)

2 Write your own historical fiction passage. Pretend you are on a covered wagon traveling west. Use one of the things you listed above to write a letter to your friend in the East.

Dear James _____ ,

We have been on the trail for six months. You would not believe

what it's like. The bumpy wagon ride makes me sick.
Sometimes I walk. We will be at our new home
soon. I'm glad!

_____

_____

Your friend,
Ana

35

CHECKOUT OPPORTUNITY

Listen to your students read individually while others work.

❶ SOUND REVIEW

❷ SHIFTY WORD BLENDING

❸ ACCURACY AND FLUENCY BUILDING

- For each task, have students say any underlined part, then read the word.
- Set a pace. Then have students read the whole words in each task and column.
- Provide repeated practice, building accuracy first, then fluency.

B1. Bossy E

Have students identify the underlined sound and then read the word.

E1. Tricky Words

- For each Tricky Word, have students use the sounds and word parts they know to silently sound out the word. Use the word in a sentence to help with pronunciation.
- If the word is unfamiliar, tell students the word.

soldier
Look at the first word. The word is *soldier*. Someone in the army is called a . . . *soldier*. Read the word three times. (soldier, solider, soldier)

earned   Todd got a job and . . . *earned* . . . money.
buys   Mom goes to the supermarket and . . . *buys* . . . food.
heard   Aimee was whispering because she did not want to be . . . *heard*.

- Have students go back and read the whole words in the column.

❹ MULTISYLLABIC WORDS

For each word, have students read the syllables, then the whole word. Use the word in a sentence, as appropriate.

company   When Leanne grows up, she wants to run her own . . . *company*.
immigrants   People who move from one country to another are . . . *immigrants*.
complete   Ronnie skipped one question. His homework wasn't . . . *complete*.
sledgehammers   The workers knocked down the wall with their . . . *sledgehammers*.
ourselves   It's important that we take care of . . . *ourselves*.
sparkle   The stones on Amber's new bracelet . . . *sparkle*.

❺ NAMES AND PLACES

- Tell students these are places and people they will read about in the story.
- Have students use the sounds and word parts they know to figure out the words. Use the words in sentences, as needed.

❻ AFFIXES

☆Have students practice reading *-ment* and the related words. Use each word in a sentence.

❼ GENERALIZATION: READING NEW WORDS IN PARAGRAPHS

- Have students read the paragraph silently, then out loud. Tell students to use the sounds and word parts they know to read any difficult words.
- Repeat practice, as needed.

☆ = New in this unit

Snapshots of the American West

Unit 15 Exercise 4
Use before Chapters 6 and 7

1. **SOUND REVIEW** Use selected Sound Cards from Units 1–15.

2. **SHIFTY WORD BLENDING** For each word, have students say the underlined part, sound out smoothly, then read the word.

grounded	pounded	sounded	sanded	landed

3. **ACCURACY/FLUENCY BUILDING** For each column, have students say any underlined part, then read each word. Next, have them read the column.

A1 Mixed Practice	B1 Bossy E	C1 Word Endings	D1 Affix Practice	E1 Tricky Words
sledge	slaves	grunts	dangerous	soldier
sweat	spikes	bosses	joyously	earned
boiled	rice	potatoes	ravenous	buys
former	states	ranchers		heard

4. **MULTISYLLABIC WORDS** Have students read each word part, then read each whole word.

Ⓐ	com·pa·ny	company	im·mi·grants	immigrants
Ⓑ	com·plete	complete	sledge·ham·mers	sledgehammers
Ⓒ	our·selves	ourselves	spark·le	sparkle

5. **NAMES AND PLACES** Have students use the sounds and words parts they know to figure out the words.

Ⓐ	California	Utah	Sierra Nevada
Ⓑ	China	Nebraska	Ming Mei (May)

6. **AFFIXES** Have students practice reading "-ment" and the related words.

★-ment	apartment	government	agreement	instrument

7. **GENERALIZATION** Have students read the paragraph silently, then out loud. (New words: Chinese, beef, sauce, fortune)

We're going to have Chinese food for dinner tonight—beef and vegetables over rice. I like lots of soy sauce on my rice. Thinking about it makes me ravenous! After dinner, Mom will give us each a fortune cookie. Then we'll take turns reading our fortunes. Next week it's Irish food. I can't wait!

MIX IT UP
(Reminder)
Response forms can be varied. Have students say the sounds using different rhythms. Have students use big voices, small voices, and deep voices. Pass the cards to students. Then have them find and return a sound. Be creative, but maintain a high rate of group responses.

26

COMPREHENSION PROCESSES

Understand, Apply

PROCEDURES

1. Introducing Vocabulary

> immigrant ☆ravenous ☆former ☆make a name for ourselves ☆hold my head up high ☆dangerous

- For each vocabulary word, have students read the word by parts, then read the whole word.
- Read the student-friendly explanations to students as they follow with their fingers. Then have students use the vocabulary word by following the gray text.
- Review and discuss the photo.

USING VOCABULARY

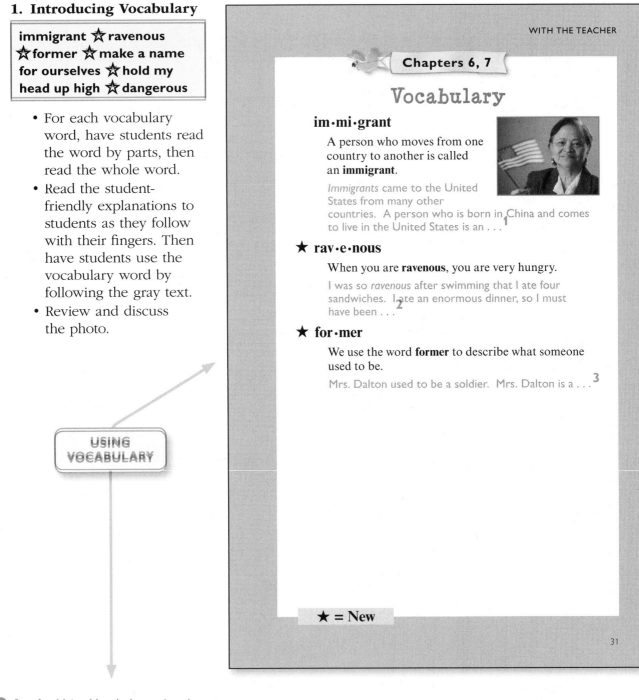

WITH THE TEACHER

Chapters 6, 7

Vocabulary

im·mi·grant

A person who moves from one country to another is called an **immigrant**.

Immigrants came to the United States from many other countries. A person who is born in China and comes to live in the United States is an . . . [1]

★ **rav·e·nous**

When you are **ravenous**, you are very hungry.

I was so ravenous after swimming that I ate four sandwiches. I ate an enormous dinner, so I must have been . . . [2]

★ **for·mer**

We use the word **former** to describe what someone used to be.

Mrs. Dalton used to be a soldier. Mrs. Dalton is a . . . [3]

★ = New

31

❶ **Apply:** Using Vocabulary—immigrant (immigrant)

❷ **Apply:** Using Vocabulary—ravenous (ravenous)

❸ **Apply:** Using Vocabulary—former (former soldier)

2. Now You Try It!

- Read or paraphrase the directions.
- Have students read the word by parts, then read the whole word.
- Have students explain or define the word in their own words. Say something like:

  Look at the word. Say the parts, then read the whole word.

  (dan•ger•ous, dangerous) Now let's pretend that we're going to explain or define the word *dangerous* to a friend. [Brett], what would you say?

  Start with "When something is *dangerous* . . ."

  (When something is dangerous, it is not safe.) That's right. Dangerous means not safe.

- Have students turn to the appropriate page in the glossary and discuss how their definition is the same as or different from the glossary's. Your students may like their definition better.

Note: By defining a word in their own words, students are demonstrating depth of word knowledge. Verbatim responses only demonstrate memorization. Encourage paraphrasing.

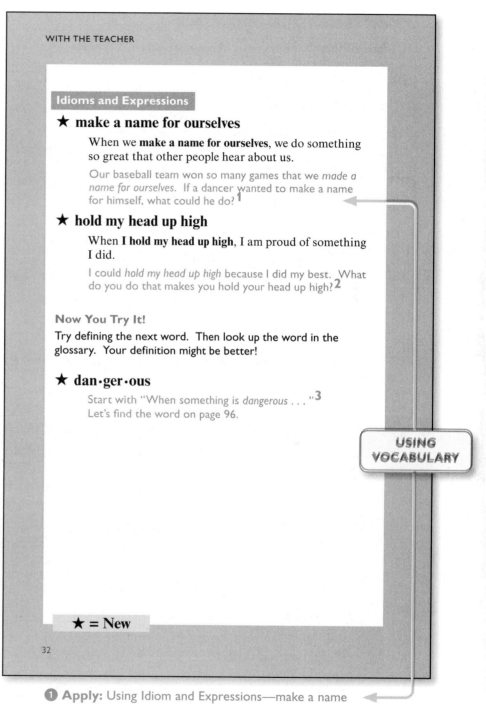

WITH THE TEACHER

Idioms and Expressions

★ **make a name for ourselves**

When we **make a name for ourselves**, we do something so great that other people hear about us.

Our baseball team won so many games that we *made a name for ourselves*. If a dancer wanted to make a name for himself, what could he do? **1**

★ **hold my head up high**

When **I hold my head up high**, I am proud of something I did.

I could *hold my head up high* because I did my best. What do you do that makes you hold your head up high? **2**

Now You Try It!

Try defining the next word. Then look up the word in the glossary. Your definition might be better!

★ **dan•ger•ous**

Start with "When something is *dangerous* . . ." **3**
Let's find the word on page 96.

★ = New

32

USING VOCABULARY

❶ Apply: Using Idiom and Expressions—make a name for ourselves (If a dancer wanted to make a name for himself, he could practice until he was the best dancer in the country.)

❷ Apply: Using Idiom and Expressions—hold my head up high (When my reading scores get better, I hold my head up high.)

❸ Understand: Defining and Using Vocabulary—dangerous; Using Glossary (When something is dangerous, it is not safe.)

CHAPTER 6 INSTRUCTIONS

Students read Chapter 6 with the teacher and Chapter 7 on their own.
Note: If you're working on an 8- to 11-Day Plan, you will read Chapter 7
with students.

COMPREHENSION PROCESSES

Remember, Understand, Apply, Analyze, Evaluate

PROCEDURES

1. Reviewing Chapter 5

Explaining; Using Vocabulary—pioneer; Inferring

Have students turn to page 28. Quickly discuss the questions from Chapter 5, Setting a
Purpose. Say something like:

Yesterday, you read Chapter 5 on your own. Let's see what you found out.

How did pioneers get wagons across a river?

(They had to take the wheels off the wagons and then put the wagons on rafts.)
What happened to the Brown family?

(Their wagon was dragged away by the river. Their wagon was lost.)
How do you think the pioneers felt when they got to a river?

(They probably thought, "Not again!" They were probably worried . . .)

2. Introducing Chapter 6

Identifying—Title; Using Graphic Organizer—Sequence; Inferring

Discuss the title and timeline. Say something like:

What's the title of this chapter? (The Great Railroad)

What years is this chapter about? (1863 to 1869)

That's right. Touch the timeline. Find when "A River Crossing" took place.

Now find 1863. Before 1863, the railroad did not go to the West, so how did people travel?

(They traveled by wagon train.)
This chapter is nonfiction. It tells how a great railroad was built from the East to the West.

Once the railroad was built, do you think people still traveled by covered wagon? (no)

Why not? (Traveling by train was easier.)

Once the railroad was built, do you think American Indians had difficulty hunting the buffalo?

(Yes, the railroad would have been in the way. There were probably too many people
around . . .)

3. First Reading

• Ask questions and discuss the story as indicated by the gray text.
• Mix group and individual turns, independent of your voice.
  Have students work toward a group accuracy goal of 0–3 errors.
  Quietly keep track of errors made by all students in the group.
• After reading the story, practice any difficult words.
  Reread the story if students have not reached the accuracy goal.

4. Second Reading, Timed Readings: Repeated Reading

• As time allows, have students do Timed Readings while others follow along.
• Time individuals for 30 seconds and encourage each child to work for a personal best.
• Determine words correct per minute. Record student scores.

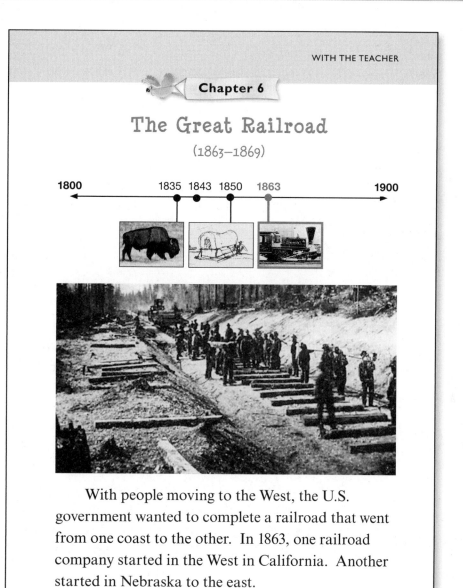

WITH THE TEACHER

Chapter 6

The Great Railroad
(1863–1869)

1800   1835 1843 1850   1863   1900

With people moving to the West, the U.S.
government wanted to complete a railroad that went
from one coast to the other. In 1863, one railroad
company started in the West in California. Another
started in Nebraska to the east.

Why do you think people wanted a railroad that went to the West?[1]

33

COMPREHENDING
AS YOU GO

❶ **Analyze:** Drawing Conclusions; **Understand:** Using Vocabulary—the West, relative
(People wanted to move, but they didn't want to go in a wagon train. The people who
moved to the West wanted their relatives to come visit them . . .)

WITH THE TEACHER

Thousands of men worked together to build the railroad. The men were Chinese and Irish immigrants, former slaves, and former soldiers.

They worked to make the ground flat, and they dug tunnels through mountains. They laid down heavy wooden ties and heavy steel rails. They pounded spikes to hold the track in place. It was hard, dangerous work, and at first they earned only one dollar a day.

In Utah on May 10, 1869, the two railroads finally met. Every worker felt proud. The new railroad would change America forever. Before, when pioneers moved to the West in wagon trains, it took many months. On a train, people could travel from coast to coast in fewer than 10 days.

The railroad made Americans feel closer to each other. They could visit people in other states, send mail quickly, and buy things from far away. Many immigrants moved out of crowded cities in the East and built farms and small towns out West. Farmers and ranchers grew more food because they could ship it to market by rail.

Describe what building the railroad was like.¹ How did the railroads change life in the United States?²

34

COMPREHENDING
AS YOU GO

❶ **Understand:** Describing; Using Vocabulary—dangerous (Building the railroad was hard dangerous work. The workers had to dig tunnels, lay down heavy steel rails, and pound spikes.)

❷ **Understand:** Explaining; Using Vocabulary—the West (The railroads made it easier for people to travel and move to the West. It was easier to buy things from far away and ship food across the country.)

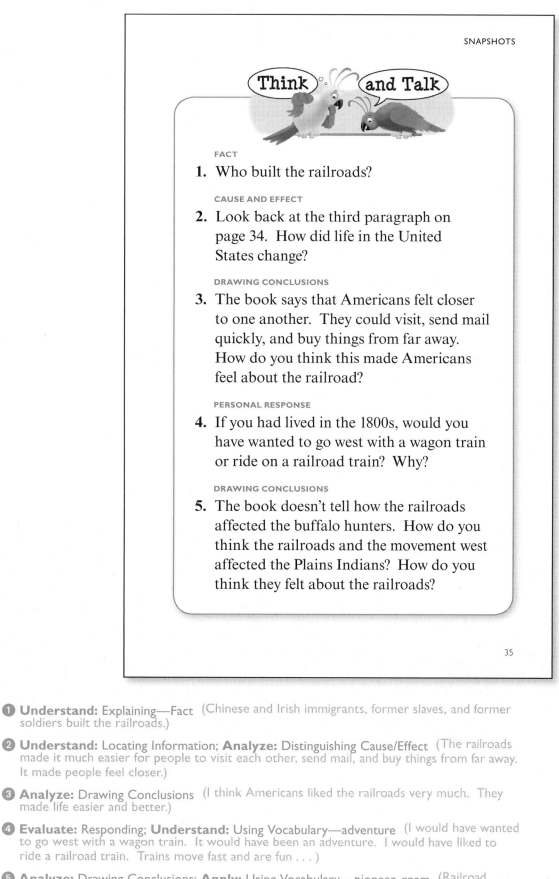

SNAPSHOTS

Think and Talk

FACT

1. Who built the railroads?

CAUSE AND EFFECT

2. Look back at the third paragraph on page 34. How did life in the United States change?

DRAWING CONCLUSIONS

3. The book says that Americans felt closer to one another. They could visit, send mail quickly, and buy things from far away. How do you think this made Americans feel about the railroad?

PERSONAL RESPONSE

4. If you had lived in the 1800s, would you have wanted to go west with a wagon train or ride on a railroad train? Why?

DRAWING CONCLUSIONS

5. The book doesn't tell how the railroads affected the buffalo hunters. How do you think the railroads and the movement west affected the Plains Indians? How do you think they felt about the railroads?

35

❶ **Understand:** Explaining—Fact (Chinese and Irish immigrants, former slaves, and former soldiers built the railroads.)

❷ **Understand:** Locating Information; **Analyze:** Distinguishing Cause/Effect (The railroads made it much easier for people to visit each other, send mail, and buy things from far away. It made people feel closer.)

❸ **Analyze:** Drawing Conclusions (I think Americans liked the railroads very much. They made life easier and better.)

❹ **Evaluate:** Responding; **Understand:** Using Vocabulary—adventure (I would have wanted to go west with a wagon train. It would have been an adventure. I would have liked to ride a railroad train. Trains move fast and are fun . . .)

❺ **Analyze:** Drawing Conclusions; **Apply:** Using Vocabulary—pioneer, roam (Railroad trains probably scared the buffalo and made it hard for the Plains Indians to hunt them. The railroads brought more pioneers, so there was less land for the buffalo to roam. The Plains Indians probably didn't like the railroads at all.)

CHAPTER 7 INSTRUCTIONS

Students read without the teacher, independently or with partners.

Note: If you're working on an 8- to 11-Day Plan, you will read Chapter 7 with students.

COMPREHENSION PROCESSES

Remember, Understand, Apply, Analyze

PROCEDURES FOR READING ON YOUR OWN

1. Getting Ready

Have students turn to Chapter 7 on page 36.

2. Introducing the Chapter and Setting a Purpose

Identifying—Title, Genre; Using Graphic Organizer—Sequence; Explaining; Inferring; Understanding Vocabulary—immigrate

Before students begin reading, say something like:

What's the title of Chapter 6? (Ming Mei, Railroad Worker)

This chapter is fiction. What does that mean?
(It's a made-up story.)

Yes, and it is historical fiction. So what does that mean?
(The story is made up, but it is about real things that happened.)

Now look at the timeline. Touch the buffalo.

What year did "Buffalo Hunt" take place? (1835)

What year did "A River Crossing" take place? (1850)

This story takes place 34 years after "Buffalo Hunt" took place and 19 years after "A River Crossing." What year does the story take place? (1869)

As you read the next pages, try to answer:
- Why did Ming Mei immigrate to the United States?
- What was it like working on the great railroad?
- Why did Ming Mei say, "We helped build America?"

> **PREP NOTE**
> **Setting a Purpose**
> Write questions on a chalkboard, white board, or large piece of paper before working with your small group.

3. Reading on Your Own: Partner or Whisper Reading

- Have students take turns reading every other page with a partner or have students whisper read on their own.
- Continue having students track each word with their fingers.
- Have students ask themselves or their partners the gray text questions.

4. Comprehension and Skill Work

For students on a 6-Day Plan, tell them they will do Timeline 1863 and 1869 and Comprehension and Skill Activity 6 after they read on their own. Guide practice, as needed. For teacher directions, see pages 75 and 76. (For 8- to 11-Day Plans, see the Lesson Planner, page 9.)

5. Homework 4: Repeated Reading

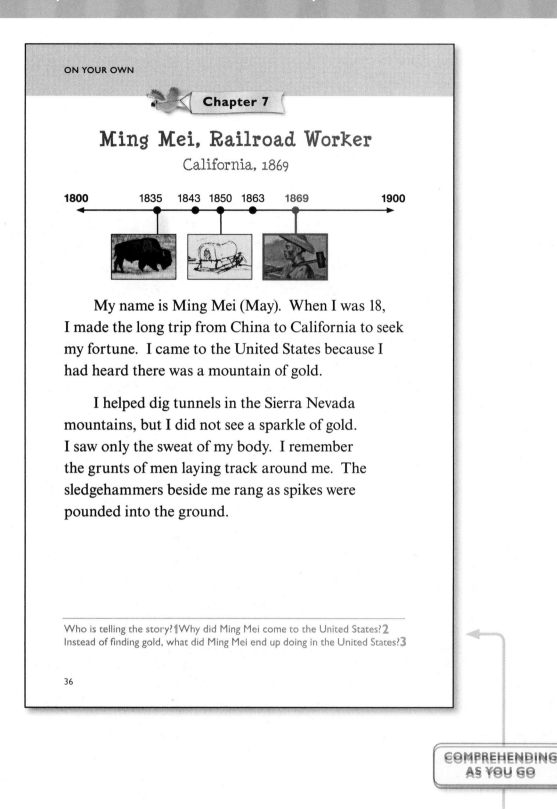

ON YOUR OWN

Chapter 7

Ming Mei, Railroad Worker
California, 1869

My name is Ming Mei (May). When I was 18, I made the long trip from China to California to seek my fortune. I came to the United States because I had heard there was a mountain of gold.

I helped dig tunnels in the Sierra Nevada mountains, but I did not see a sparkle of gold. I saw only the sweat of my body. I remember the grunts of men laying track around me. The sledgehammers beside me rang as spikes were pounded into the ground.

Who is telling the story?**1** Why did Ming Mei come to the United States?**2**
Instead of finding gold, what did Ming Mei end up doing in the United States?**3**

36

COMPREHENDING
AS YOU GO

1 **Remember:** Identifying—Narrator (Ming Mei is telling the story.)
2 **Understand:** Explaining (Ming Mei came to the United States to seek his fortune and find gold.)
3 **Understand:** Explaining (Ming Mei helped build the railroad.)

SNAPSHOTS

There were many Chinese workers laying tracks. We worked hard. We made a fine name for ourselves in this country. As we worked, I saw miles of perfect railroad tracks behind us. I held my head up high.

The mountains were beautiful, but the air was bitter cold. We were ravenous after a hard day's work. We ate fish with soy sauce, rice, and vegetables. Our food and tea made us strong. It reminded us of our old home in China.

There were also many Irish workers. The Irish had to eat what the bosses gave them—boiled beef and potatoes every day. Nothing else. They were often sick from this food or from the water they drank.

After working on the rails, why did Ming Mei *hold his head up high?***1** What made the Chinese workers strong?**2** Who else helped build the railroads?**3** How was their food different from Ming Mei's?**4**

37

COMPREHENDING AS YOU GO

❶ Apply: Inferring; Explaining; Using Idioms and Expressions—hold my head up high (Ming Mei held his head up high because he was proud of the railroad tracks he helped build.)

❷ Remember: Identifying—What (Their food and tea made them strong.)

❸ Remember: Identifying—Who (Irish workers also helped build the railroad.)

❹ Analyze: Contrasting (The Irish had boiled beef and potatoes. The Chinese workers ate fish, rice, and vegetables.)

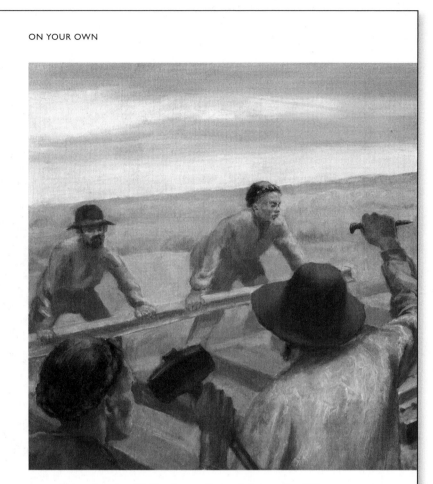

One day in 1869, the railroad from the West met up with the railroad from the East. We had built an amazing thing—a railroad that reached all the way across the country.

38

SNAPSHOTS

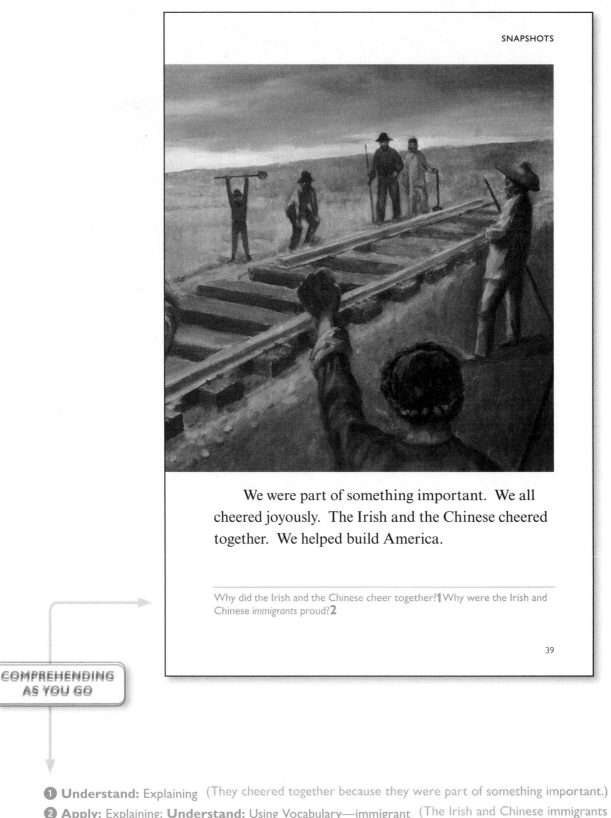

We were part of something important. We all cheered joyously. The Irish and the Chinese cheered together. We helped build America.

Why did the Irish and the Chinese cheer together?**1** Why were the Irish and Chinese *immigrants* proud?**2**

39

COMPREHENDING AS YOU GO

❶ Understand: Explaining (They cheered together because they were part of something important.)

❷ Apply: Explaining; **Understand:** Using Vocabulary—immigrant (The Irish and Chinese immigrants were proud because they helped build America.)

1863 • THE GREAT RAILROAD AND 1869 • MING MEI

COMPREHENSION PROCESSES
Understand, Apply, Analyze, Create

WRITING TRAITS
Conventions—Complete Sentence, Capital, Period

Using Graphic Organizer
Viewing; Illustrating; Generating Ideas
Sentence Writing

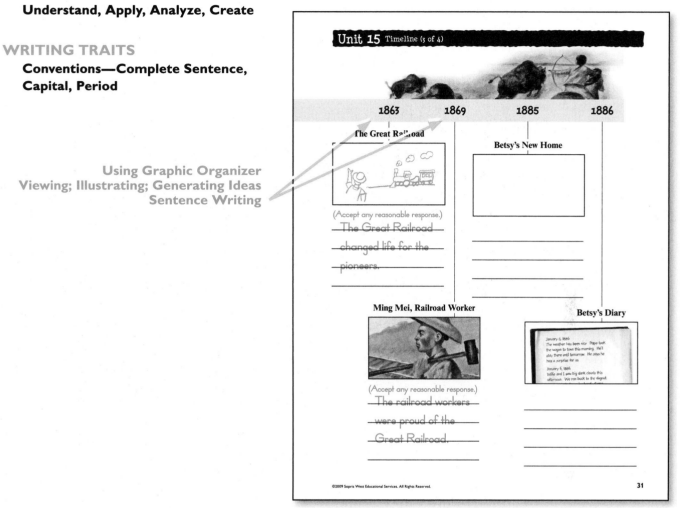

Unit 15 Timeline (3 of 4)

| 1863 | 1869 | 1885 | 1886 |

The Great Railroad

(Accept any reasonable response.)
The Great Railroad changed life for the pioneers.

Betsy's New Home

Ming Mei, Railroad Worker

(Accept any reasonable response.)
The railroad workers were proud of the Great Railroad.

Betsy's Diary

January 5, 1886
The weather has been nice. Papa took the wagon to town this morning. He'll stay there until tomorrow. He says he has a surprise for us.

January 6, 1886
Willie and I saw big dark clouds this afternoon. We ran back to the dugout.

31

PROCEDURES
Have students complete the page independently. Guide practice, only as needed.

Timeline: Sequencing, Caption Writing—Specific Instructions
- Under 1863, have students draw a picture to illustrate "The Great Railroad," then write a short caption for their picture.
- Have students look at the picture under 1869, then write a short caption about "Ming Mei, Railroad Worker."
- Remind them to use a complete sentence, capitals, and a period.

MAZE READING AND STORY COMPREHENSION, VOCABULARY AND SYNONYMS

COMPREHENSION PROCESSES
Understand, Apply

WRITING TRAITS
Period

PROCEDURES
For each step, demonstrate and guide practice, as needed. Then have students complete the page independently.

Maze Reading—Basic Instructions
- Have students read the sentences and select the word in parentheses that best completes the sentence.
- Have students circle the word, then reread the paragraph to make sure the whole paragraph makes sense.

Vocabulary and Synonyms: Selection Response—Basic Instructions (Items 1–4)
- Have students read the boxed paragraph.
- Have students fill in the bubbles and blanks with the correct word choice. Remind them to put a period at the end of a sentence, where needed.

Self-monitoring
Have students check and correct their work.

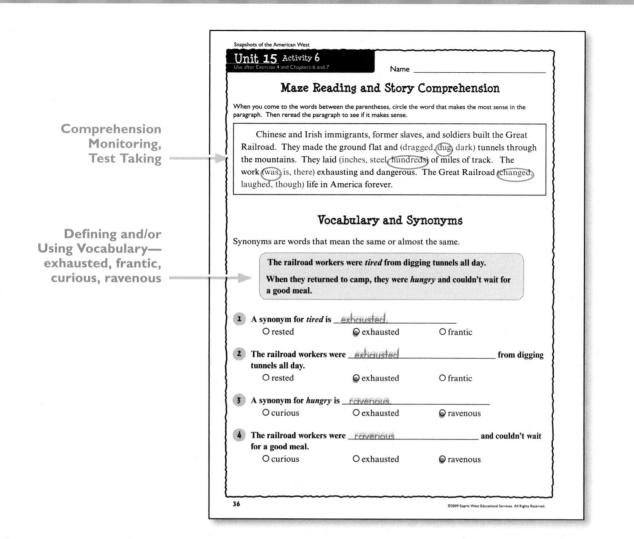

Comprehension Monitoring, Test Taking

Defining and/or Using Vocabulary— exhausted, frantic, curious, ravenous

Snapshots of the American West

Unit 15 Activity 6
Use after Exercise 4 and Chapters 6 and 7

Name _____

Maze Reading and Story Comprehension

When you come to the words between the parentheses, circle the word that makes the most sense in the paragraph. Then reread the paragraph to see if it makes sense.

Chinese and Irish immigrants, former slaves, and soldiers built the Great Railroad. They made the ground flat and (dragged, dug, dark) tunnels through the mountains. They laid (inches, steel, hundreds) of miles of track. The work (was, is, there) exhausting and dangerous. The Great Railroad (changed, laughed, though) life in America forever.

Vocabulary and Synonyms

Synonyms are words that mean the same or almost the same.

> The railroad workers were *tired* from digging tunnels all day.
>
> When they returned to camp, they were *hungry* and couldn't wait for a good meal.

1 A synonym for *tired* is ___exhausted.___
　　○ rested　　　　◉ exhausted　　　○ frantic

2 The railroad workers were ___exhausted___ from digging tunnels all day.
　　○ rested　　　　◉ exhausted　　　○ frantic

3 A synonym for *hungry* is ___ravenous.___
　　○ curious　　　○ exhausted　　　◉ ravenous

4 The railroad workers were ___ravenous___ and couldn't wait for a good meal.
　　○ curious　　　○ exhausted　　　◉ ravenous

36　　　　　　　　　　　　　　　　©2009 Sopris West Educational Services. All Rights Reserved.

❶ SOUND REVIEW
Use selected Sound Cards from Units 1–15.

❷ SHIFTY WORD BLENDING
For each word, have students say the underlined sound. Then have them sound out the word smoothly and say it. Use the words in sentences, as appropriate.

❸ ACCURACY AND FLUENCY BUILDING
- For each task, have students say any underlined part, then read the word.
- Set a pace. Then have students read the whole words in each task and column.
- Provide repeated practice, building accuracy first, then fluency.

C1. Morphographs and Affixes
Have students read the underlined part, then the whole word.

E1. Tricky Words
- For each Tricky Word, have students use the sounds and word parts they know to silently sound out the word. Use the word in a sentence to help with pronunciation.
- If the word is unfamiliar, tell students the word.

prairie

Look at the first word. Sound the word out silently. Thumbs up when you know the word. Use my sentence to help you pronounce the word. The cows wandered the open . . . *prairie.* Read the word three times. (prairie, prairie, prairie)

ceiling	Nan saw a spider crawling across the . . . *ceiling.*
putting	I'm moving your pencil. I'm . . . *putting* . . . it here.
answered	Carmen asked a question, but nobody . . . *answered.*
thought	I took your book by mistake. I . . . *thought* . . . it was mine.
brought	"Yum, this salad is good," said Jude. "Who . . . *brought* . . . it?"

- Have students go back and read the whole words in the column.

❹ CONTRACTIONS
Have students read the first two words, then the contraction.

❺ MULTISYLLABIC WORDS
For each word, have students read the syllables, then the whole word. Use the word in a sentence, as appropriate.

regular	The bus was late. It didn't come at its . . . *regular* . . . time.
settler	Someone who makes a home where few people live is a . . . *settler.*
secret	Don't tell anyone. It's a . . . *secret.*
bacon	For breakfast, Jaime likes eggs and . . . *bacon.*

❻ GENERALIZATION: READING NEW WORDS IN PARAGRAPHS
- Have students read the paragraph silently, then out loud. Tell students to use the sounds and word parts they know to read any difficult words.
- Repeat practice, as needed.

Snapshots of the American West

Unit 15 Exercise 5
Use before Chapters 8 and 9

1. SOUND REVIEW Use selected Sound Cards from Units 1–15.

2. SHIFTY WORD BLENDING For each word, have students say the underlined part, sound out smoothly, then read the word.

| r<u>a</u>ce | <u>br</u>ace | bra<u>ve</u> | <u>gr</u>ave | <u>c</u>ave |

3. ACCURACY/FLUENCY BUILDING For each column, have students say any underlined part, then read each word. Next, have them read the column.

A1 Mixed Practice	**B1** Compound Words	**C1** Morphographs & Affixes	**D1** Word Endings	**E1** Tricky Words
st<u>o</u>ve	dugout	dange<u>rous</u>	<u>nod</u>ded	prairie
ox<u>en</u>	farmhouse	act<u>or</u>	<u>scr</u>atching	ceiling
b<u>ur</u>n	floorboards	govern<u>ment</u>	<u>th</u>umping	putting
cl<u>ou</u>ds	**B2** Names and Places	<u>di</u>stance	self	answered
<u>c</u>enter	Willie		selves	thought
sett<u>ler</u>	January		wolf	brought
bu<u>ck</u>et	Indiana		wolves	

4. CONTRACTIONS Have students read the words, then the contraction.

| he + would = he'd | where + is = where's |

5. MULTISYLLABIC WORDS Have students read each word part, then read each whole word.

| Ⓐ | reg•u•lar | regular | set•tler | settler |
| Ⓑ | se•cret | secret | ba•con | bacon |

6. GENERALIZATION Have students read the paragraph silently, then out loud. (New words: diary, piano, Irma)

Dear Diary,

We moved into our new farmhouse yesterday. It is great. We put all of our belongings in the wagon—even the piano. Then we drove to the new house. Finally, we unloaded everything. It was hard work, but we love our new house.

Irma

27

COMPREHENSION PROCESSES
Understand, Apply

PROCEDURES

1. Introducing Vocabulary

☆ **prairie** ☆ **dugout** ☆ **settler, embarrassed**

- For each vocabulary word, have students read the word by parts, then read the whole word.
- Read the student-friendly explanations to students as they follow with their fingers. Then have students use the vocabulary word by following the gray text.
- Review and discuss the photos and illustrations.

2. Now You Try It!

- Read or paraphrase the directions.
- Have students read the word by parts, then read the whole word.
- Have students explain or define the word in their own words.
- Have students turn to the appropriate page in the glossary and discuss how their definition is the same as or different from the glossary's. Your students may like their definition better.

Note: By defining a word in their own words, students are demonstrating depth of word knowledge. Verbatim responses only demonstrate memorization. Encourage paraphrasing.

☆ = New in this unit

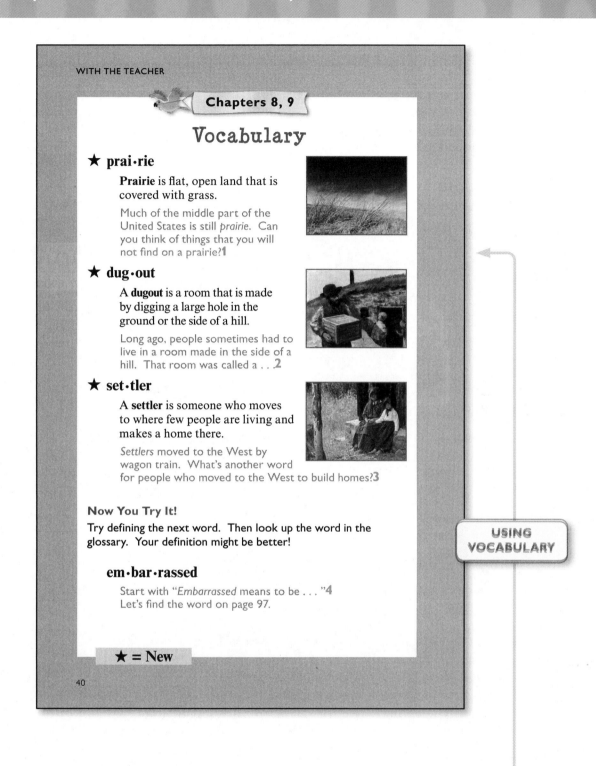

WITH THE TEACHER

Chapters 8, 9

Vocabulary

★ **prai·rie**

Prairie is flat, open land that is covered with grass.

Much of the middle part of the United States is still *prairie*. Can you think of things that you will not find on a prairie?**1**

★ **dug·out**

A **dugout** is a room that is made by digging a large hole in the ground or the side of a hill.

Long ago, people sometimes had to live in a room made in the side of a hill. That room was called a . . .**2**

★ **set·tler**

A **settler** is someone who moves to where few people are living and makes a home there.

Settlers moved to the West by wagon train. What's another word for people who moved to the West to build homes?**3**

Now You Try It!
Try defining the next word. Then look up the word in the glossary. Your definition might be better!

em·bar·rassed

Start with "*Embarrassed* means to be . . ."**4** Let's find the word on page 97.

★ = New

40

USING VOCABULARY

1 Apply: Inferring; **Understand:** Using Vocabulary—prairie (You will not find trees or buildings on a prairie.)

2 Understand: Using Vocabulary—dugout (dugout)

3 Understand: Using Vocabulary—settler, the West (Settlers is another word for the people who moved to the West to build homes.)

4 Understand: Defining and Using Vocabulary—embarrassed; Using Glossary (Embarrassed means to be uncomfortable or nervous and worried about something you have done or said.)

CHAPTER 8 INSTRUCTIONS

Students read Chapter 8 with the teacher and Chapter 9 on their own.

COMPREHENSION PROCESSES

Remember, Understand, Apply, Analyze, Evaluate, Create

PROCEDURES

1. Reviewing Chapter 7

Summarizing

Have students turn to page 36. Quickly discuss the questions from Chapter 7, Setting a Purpose. Say something like:

Yesterday, you read Chapter 7 on your own. Let's see what you found out.

Why did Ming Mei immigrate to the United States? (He thought he would find a mountain of gold.)

What was it like working on the great railroad? (It was very hard work. The workers laid track, pounded nails, used sledgehammers . . .)

Why did Ming Mei say, "We helped build America?" (He was proud of his work.)

2. Introducing Chapter 8

Identifying—Title, Setting; Using Graphic Organizer—Sequence

Discuss the title and the timeline. Say something like:

Turn to page 41. What's the title of this chapter? (Betsy's New Home)

Look at the subtitle. Where does this story take place? (Nebraska)

When does it take place? (1885)

Look at the timeline, what were some of the stories that took place before this?

(Buffalo Hunt, A River Crossing, Ming Mei . . .)

This story takes place after the great buffalo hunts, after many wagon trains had gone west, and after the great railroad from the East to the West had been built.

> **REPEATED READINGS**
> **Prosody**
>
> On the second reading, students practice developing prosody—phrasing and expression. Research has shown that prosody is related to both fluency and comprehension.

3. First Reading

- Ask questions and discuss the text as indicated by the gray text.
- Mix group and individual turns, independent of your voice.
  Have students work toward a group accuracy goal of 0–5 errors.
  Quietly keep track of errors made by all students in the group.
- After reading the story, practice any difficult words.
  Repeat, if students have not reached the accuracy goal.

4. Second Reading, Short Passage Practice: Developing Prosody

- Demonstrate expressive, fluent reading of the first paragraph. Read at a rate slightly faster than the students' rate. Say something like:
- Guide practice with your voice.
- Provide individual turns while others track with their fingers and whisper read.
- Repeat with one paragraph at a time.

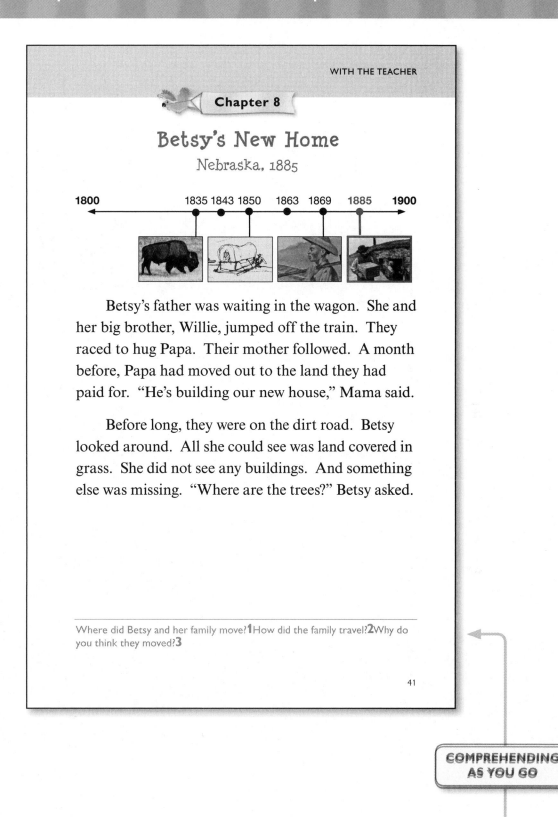

Chapter 8

Betsy's New Home

Nebraska, 1885

1800 ········· 1835 1843 1850 ···· 1863 ··· 1869 ···· 1885 ··· **1900**

Betsy's father was waiting in the wagon. She and her big brother, Willie, jumped off the train. They raced to hug Papa. Their mother followed. A month before, Papa had moved out to the land they had paid for. "He's building our new house," Mama said.

Before long, they were on the dirt road. Betsy looked around. All she could see was land covered in grass. She did not see any buildings. And something else was missing. "Where are the trees?" Betsy asked.

Where did Betsy and her family move?**1** How did the family travel?**2** Why do you think they moved?**3**

41

COMPREHENDING AS YOU GO

1 Apply: Inferring—Where (Betsy and her family moved west to Nebraska.)

2 Remember: Identifying—Action (They rode on the train.)

3 Apply: Inferring (They wanted a new and better home. They wanted a better life. They wanted to own their own land.)

WITH THE TEACHER

"This is the prairie," Willie answered. "There aren't many trees out here." This made Betsy sad. She liked the big trees around their farmhouse in Indiana. But now they had moved to Nebraska—600 miles away.

Finally, Papa stopped the oxen. They were on top of a small hill. Betsy saw a creek nearby. "Here we are," Papa said.

Betsy was excited. "Where's the house?" she asked.

Papa chuckled. "You're standing on it," he said. He and Willie began unloading boxes from the wagon. They also unloaded two glass windows and a door.

How was Betsy's old home in Indiana different from her new home? **1**

42

COMPREHENDING
AS YOU GO

1 **Analyze:** Contrasting; **Understand:** Using Vocabulary—prairie (Her old home in Indiana had big trees around it. Her new home was on the prairie where there weren't many trees.)

SNAPSHOTS

Betsy and her mother walked down the hill. There were two small windows in the side of the hill. They did not have any glass in them. Between them was a doorway without a door.

Betsy looked up at Mama. "Is that our house?" she asked.

Mama nodded and smiled. "It's called a dugout."

Betsy peeked inside. It was dark and smelled like dirt. The walls were dirt, and the floor was dirt. A small wood stove stood in the corner. In the center was their old table. They were going to live inside the hill!

Why do you think Betsy's father made a *dugout* for a home?[1] Do you think Betsy will like living inside the hill?[2]

43

COMPREHENDING
AS YOU GO

❶ Analyze: Drawing Conclusions; **Understand:** Using Vocabulary—prairie, dugout (There weren't many trees on the prairie, so he couldn't use wood to make a house. Betsy's dad had to make a dugout because there wasn't anything else to build a house with.)
❷ Apply: Predicting (No, it will be dirty and dark. Yes, it will be an adventure . . .)

Mama found a bucket. "Betsy, please fetch some water from the creek," Mama said.

When Betsy got back, Papa and Willie were already putting in the windows. Then they hung the door in the doorway. Mama had a fire going in the stove. Betsy could smell a yummy pot of pork and beans.

They sat down for dinner. A chunk of dirt fell from the ceiling. It landed in Papa's empty bowl. They all laughed. But Papa looked a little embarrassed.

"Next year, we'll build a regular house," he said, "after we get the crops planted."

"Can we plant trees too?" Betsy asked.

Papa smiled and gave her a wink. "We sure can," he said.

44

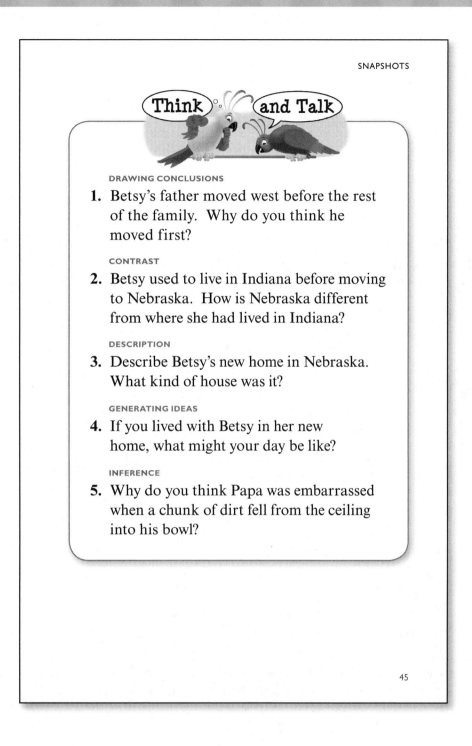

SNAPSHOTS

Think and Talk

DRAWING CONCLUSIONS

1. Betsy's father moved west before the rest of the family. Why do you think he moved first?

CONTRAST

2. Betsy used to live in Indiana before moving to Nebraska. How is Nebraska different from where she had lived in Indiana?

DESCRIPTION

3. Describe Betsy's new home in Nebraska. What kind of house was it?

GENERATING IDEAS

4. If you lived with Betsy in her new home, what might your day be like?

INFERENCE

5. Why do you think Papa was embarrassed when a chunk of dirt fell from the ceiling into his bowl?

45

❶ Analyze: Drawing Conclusions (He wanted to build the house and have it ready for his family. Moving first and getting the house ready made it easier for everyone else.)

❷ Analyze: Contrasting (Indiana had big trees, but in Nebraska, there weren't many trees.)

❸ Understand: Describing; Using Vocabulary—dugout (Her new home was a dugout. It was inside a hill, so the walls and floor were made of dirt, and it was dark.)

❹ Create: Generating Ideas; **Evaluate:** Responding (I would build a fire first thing in the morning to cook breakfast. Later, I would work in the garden and bring in fresh vegetables for dinner. I would sweep the floor to keep the dirt out. I would go to bed early because there were no lights or TV . . .)

❺ Apply: Inferring; **Understand:** Using Vocabulary—embarrassed (He was embarrassed because he made the house, and he wanted it to be good for his family. He was embarrassed because the dugout wasn't a very nice home.)

CHAPTER 9 INSTRUCTIONS

Students read without the teacher, independently or with partners.

COMPREHENSION PROCESSES

Understand

PROCEDURES FOR READING ON YOUR OWN

1. Getting Ready

Have students turn to Chapter 9 on page 46.

2. Setting a Purpose

Identifying—Title, What; Classifying—Genre

Before students begin reading, say something like:

What's the title of Chapter 9? (Betsy's Diary)

A diary is like a journal. A diary is a book that people write in. People tell what's happening in their lives in a diary.

"Betsy's Diary" was written recently, but it is about real things that happened in the lives of people in the 1880s.

Look at the first date in Betsy's Diary. What does it say? (January 5, 1886)

"Betsy's Diary" includes events that took place during the winter after her family had lived in the dugout for several months. Winters in Nebraska are very cold.

Do you think this story is fiction or nonfiction? (fiction)

What kind of fiction? (historical)

Yes, just like many of the other chapters in this story, "Betsy's Diary" is historical fiction.

Read to find out the answers to these questions:
- What happened on January 6?
- How did Betsy's family keep the chickens safe?
- What was the family worried about from January 7 to January 12?
- What did the family have to be thankful for?

> **PREP NOTE**
>
> **Setting a Purpose**
> Write questions on a chalkboard, white board, or large piece of paper before working with your small group.

3. Reading on Your Own: Partner or Whisper Reading
- Have students take turns reading every other page with a partner or have students whisper read on their own.
- Continue having students track each word with their fingers.

4. Comprehension and Skill Work

For students on a 6-Day Plan, tell them they will do Timeline 1885 and 1886 and Comprehension and Skill Activity 7 after they read on their own. Guide practice, as needed. For teacher directions, see pages 92 and 93.

5. Homework 5: Repeated Reading

WITH THE TEACHER

Chapter 9

Betsy's Diary
California, 1869

1800   1835   1843   1850   1863   1869   1885   1886   1900

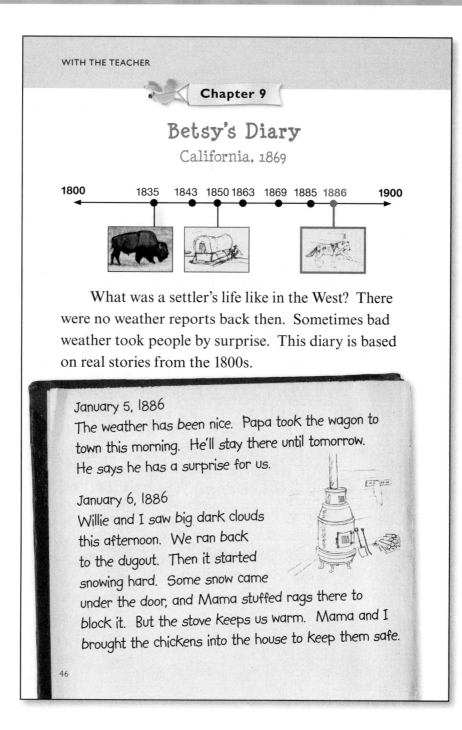

What was a settler's life like in the West? There were no weather reports back then. Sometimes bad weather took people by surprise. This diary is based on real stories from the 1800s.

January 5, 1886

The weather has been nice. Papa took the wagon to town this morning. He'll stay there until tomorrow. He says he has a surprise for us.

January 6, 1886

Willie and I saw big dark clouds this afternoon. We ran back to the dugout. Then it started snowing hard. Some snow came under the door, and Mama stuffed rags there to block it. But the stove keeps us warm. Mama and I brought the chickens into the house to keep them safe.

46

January 7, 1886

It's snowing so hard that you can't see very far. And the snow is getting very deep outside. Willie had to go to the shed to feed and milk Irma, our cow. We tied a rope around his middle so he wouldn't get lost. When he came back, he was covered in snow. He looked like a snowman! But he had a bucket of warm milk. Mama says she's worried about Papa. I am too. I'm worried he got caught in the snowstorm.

January 9, 1886

The snow finally stopped, but it's really cold outside. We have plenty of potatoes and bacon to eat. And we still have some wood for the fire.

January 10, 1886

Last night we heard scratching at the door. At first we thought maybe it was Papa. But this morning we saw wolf tracks outside. I'm not scared. Papa says I'm brave. But I sure wish he'd come home.

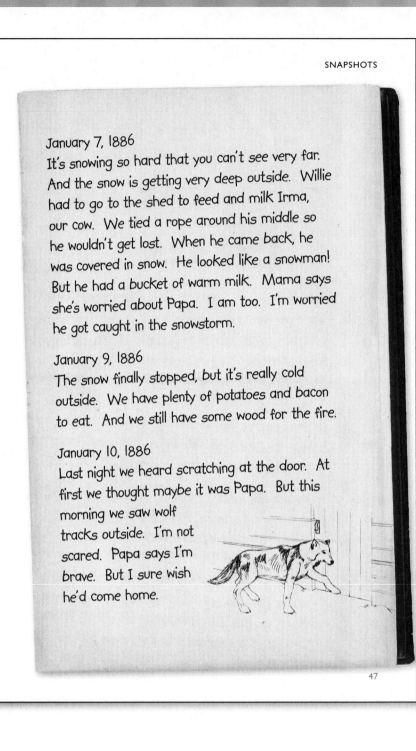

47

ON YOUR OWN

January 11, 1886
We ran out of wood so we had to burn some floorboards this morning. Now I'm a little scared.

January 12, 1886
This morning we stayed in bed to keep warm. We heard thumping on the roof. I thought maybe the wolves were back. Then we heard footsteps. A big snowman appeared in the doorway. It was Papa!

January 13, 1886
I asked Papa about the surprise. He said we would get the secret when the snow melted. Then Papa whispered, "Can you keep a secret?" I nodded. Papa whispered, "It's a piano. I got your Mama and you a piano."

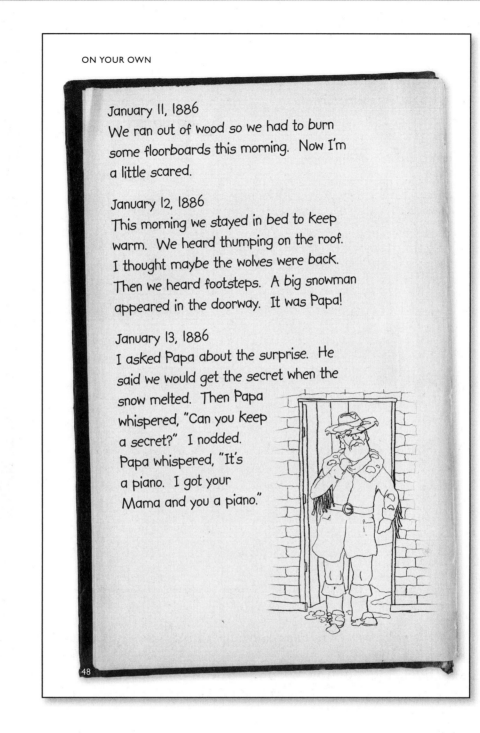

48

1885 • BETSY'S NEW HOME AND 1886 • BETSY'S DIARY

COMPREHENSION PROCESSES

Understand, Apply, Analyze, Create

WRITING TRAITS

Conventions—Complete Sentence, Capital, Period

Using Graphic Organizer
Viewing; Illustrating; Generating Ideas
Sentence Writing

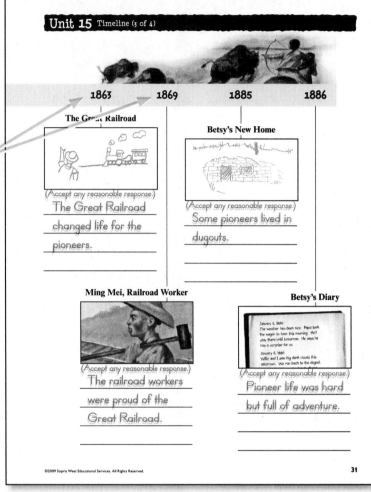

Unit 15 Timeline (3 of 4)

1863   1869   1885   1886

The Great Railroad

(Accept any reasonable response.)
The Great Railroad changed life for the pioneers.

Betsy's New Home

(Accept any reasonable response.)
Some pioneers lived in dugouts.

Ming Mei, Railroad Worker

(Accept any reasonable response.)
The railroad workers were proud of the Great Railroad.

Betsy's Diary

January 5, 1886
The weather has been nice. Papa took the wagon to town this morning. He'll stay there until tomorrow. He says he has a surprise for us.

January 6, 1886
Willie and I saw big dark clouds this afternoon. We ran back to the dugout.

(Accept any reasonable response.)
Pioneer life was hard but full of adventure.

31

PROCEDURES

Have students complete the page independently. Guide practice, only as needed.

Timeline: Sequencing, Caption Writing—Specific Instructions

• Under 1885, have students draw a picture to illustrate "Betsy's New Home," then write a short caption about their picture.

• Have students look at the picture under 1886, then write a short caption about "Betsy's Diary."

• Remind them to use a complete sentence, capitals, and a period.

Note: Have students finish the back cover of the Timeline folder and take it home.

PASSAGE COMPREHENSION

COMPREHENSION PROCESSES

Understand Apply, Evaluate, Create

WRITING TRAITS

Period

Snapshots of the American West

Unit 15 Activity 7
Use after Exercise 5 and Chapters 8 and 9

Name _____

Passage Comprehension

Sod Houses

When the pioneers headed west, many people built new homes on the prairie. A prairie is like a sea of grass. There are very few trees. With no trees, most pioneers had no wood to build their new homes. The pioneers used what was there. Many people built their first homes of grass and dirt. The houses were called sod houses.

Sod houses were usually just one room. They were dark and damp. When it rained, the sod houses leaked, and the dirt floors turned into mud. The pioneers shared their homes with mice, snakes, and all kinds of insects.

Identifying—Topic →
1. This passage is about _sod houses._

Defining and Using Vocabulary—prairie →
2. Describe a prairie. A prairie is _like a sea of grass._

Inferring, Explaining →
3. What is sod? Sod is _grass and dirt._

Responding, Generating Ideas →
4. I _would not_ want to live in a sod house because
   ~~would~~ (would not)
   it would be dark and damp. I would not like to live with mice
   and snakes.

©2009 Sopris West Educational Services. All Rights Reserved.   37

PROCEDURES

For each step, demonstrate and guide practice, as needed. Then have students complete the page independently.

Sentence Completion—Basic Instructions (Items 1–4)
Have students read the passage, then the sentence starters. Have them write answers that correctly complete the sentences. Remind students to put a period at the end of sentences.

Self-monitoring
Have students check and correct their work.

❶ SOUND REVIEW

❷ ACCURACY AND FLUENCY BUILDING
- For each task, have students say any underlined part, then read the word.
- Set a pace. Then have students read the whole words in each task and column.
- Provide repeated practice, building accuracy first, then fluency.

C1. Multisyllabic Words
- For the list of words divided by syllables, have students read each syllable, then the whole word. Use the word in a sentence, as appropriate.
- For the list of whole words, build accuracy and then fluency.

rely	I trust my parents. I can . . . *rely* . . . on them.
former	Dan used to be president of the club. Dan is the . . . *former* . . . president.
photography	Taking pictures with a camera is called . . . *photography.*
adventure	Miss Tam went on an African . . . *adventure.*
buckets	We went to the well and filled up our . . . *buckets.*
reservations	Many American Indians live on . . . *reservations.*
purpose	The reason we go to school is to learn. That's our . . . *purpose.*
essay	My sister wrote a paper about the building of the railroad. Her paper is called an . . . *essay.*

E1. Tricky Words
- For each Tricky Word, have students use the sounds and word parts they know to silently sound out the word. Use the word in a sentence to help with pronunciation.

cradleboard

Look at the first word. Say the word parts silently. Thumbs up when you know the word. Use my sentence to help you pronounce the word. The baby was warm and secure in its . . . *cradleboard.* Read the word two times. (cradleboard, cradleboard)

piece	Neil likes the cake. He wants another . . . *piece.*
prairies	Flat areas of wide open land are called . . . *prairies.*
journeyed	Pioneers in wagon trains . . . *journeyed* . . . west.
created	Zadi drew that picture. She . . . *created* it.

- Have students go back and read the whole words in the column.

❸ WORD ENDINGS

❹ PLACES
- Tell students these are places they will read about in the story.
- Have students use the sounds and word parts they know to figure out the words. Use the words in sentences, as needed.

❺ MORPHOGRAPHS AND AFFIXES
- Have students read "-*or* equals one who" and the accompanying word and sentence.
- Then have students explain the sentence.
- For Rows B and C, have students read the underlined part, then the word.
- Repeat practice with whole words, mixing group and individual turns.
  Build accuracy, then fluency.

Snapshots of the American West

Unit 15 Exercise 6
Use before Chapter 10

1. **SOUND REVIEW** Have students review sounds for accuracy, then for fluency.

A	ew as in crew	ph as in phone	au as in astronaut	ce as in center	-y as in fly
B	ue	kn	oy	gi	oi

2. **ACCURACY/FLUENCY BUILDING** For each column, have students say any underlined part, then read each word. Next, have them read the column.

A1 Mixed Practice	**B1** Compound Words	**C1** Multisyllabic Words		**D1** Tricky Words
r<u>ai</u>se	homestead	re•ly	rely	cradleboard
r<u>o</u>de	background	form•er	former	piece
<u>a</u>side	firewood	pho•tog•raph•y	photography	prairies
lives	steamboat	ad•ven•ture	adventure	journeyed
dr<u>y</u>ing		buck•ets	buckets	created
		res•er•va•tions	reservations	
		pur•pose	purpose	
		es•say	essay	

MONITORING PROGRESS

For all activities, mix group and individual turns to keep students engaged and to monitor individual performance.

3. **WORD ENDINGS** Have students read each word set.

A	community	communities	family	families
B	change	changing	carry	carried

4. **PLACES** Have students use the sounds and word parts they know to figure out the words.

Kansas	Cheyenne	Montana	Oklahoma	St. Louis

5. **MORPHOGRAPHS AND AFFIXES** Have students practice reading "-or = one who" and the related word and sentence. For rows B and C, have students read each underlined part, then the word.

A	-or = one who	collector = one who collects	The coin <u>collector</u> looks for coins in the park.	
B	cur<u>ious</u>	<u>dis</u>play	<u>de</u>scribe	<u>ex</u>pect
C	apart<u>ment</u>	tradition<u>al</u>	flex<u>ible</u>	<u>re</u>play

28

COMPREHENSION PROCESSES
Remember, Understand, Apply

PROCEDURES

1. Introducing Vocabulary

> ☆Cheyenne ☆reservation,
> former ☆homestead
> ☆rely, community,
> belongings

- For each vocabulary word, have students read the word by parts, then read the whole word.
- Read the student-friendly explanations to students as they follow with their fingers. Then have students use the vocabulary word by following the gray text.
- Review and discuss the photos.

> **USING VOCABULARY**

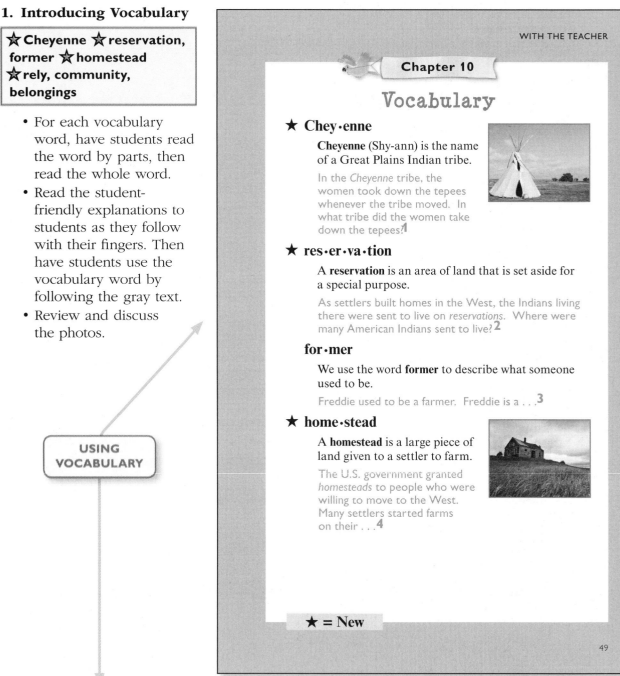

WITH THE TEACHER

Chapter 10

Vocabulary

★ **Chey·enne**

Cheyenne (Shy-ann) is the name of a Great Plains Indian tribe.

In the *Cheyenne* tribe, the women took down the tepees whenever the tribe moved. In what tribe did the women take down the tepees?[1]

★ **res·er·va·tion**

A **reservation** is an area of land that is set aside for a special purpose.

As settlers built homes in the West, the Indians living there were sent to live on *reservations*. Where were many American Indians sent to live?[2]

for·mer

We use the word **former** to describe what someone used to be.

Freddie used to be a farmer. Freddie is a . . .[3]

★ **home·stead**

A **homestead** is a large piece of land given to a settler to farm.

The U.S. government granted *homesteads* to people who were willing to move to the West. Many settlers started farms on their . . .[4]

★ = New

49

❶ **Remember:** Using Vocabulary—Cheyenne, tribe (The women in the Cheyenne tribe took down the tepees.)

❷ **Understand:** Using Vocabulary—reservation (American Indians were sent to live on reservations.)

❸ **Apply:** Using Vocabulary—former (former farmer)

❹ **Apply:** Using Vocabulary—homestead (homestead)

2. Now You Try It!

- Read or paraphrase the directions.
- For each word, have students read the word by parts, then read the whole word.
- Have students explain or define the word in their own words. Say something like:

  Look at the word. Say the parts, then read the whole word.

  (com•mun•i•ty, community) Now, let's pretend that we're going to explain or define the word *community* to a friend. [Murray], what would you say?

  Start with "A *community* is a . . ." (A community is a group of people living in the same area.)

  That's right. A community is a group of people living in the same area.

- Have students turn to the appropriate page in the glossary and discuss how their definitions are the same as or different from the glossary's. Your students may like their definitions better.

Note: By defining a word in their own words, students are demonstrating depth of word knowledge. Verbatim responses only demonstrate memorization. Encourage paraphrasing.

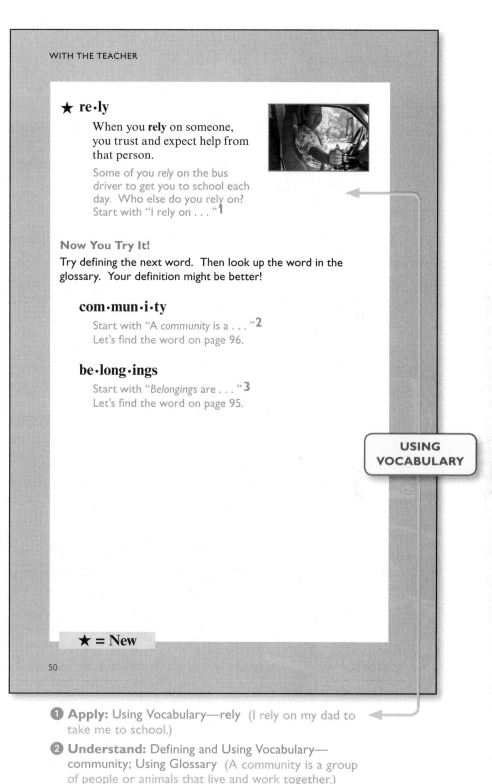

WITH THE TEACHER

★ re·ly

When you **rely** on someone, you trust and expect help from that person.

Some of you rely on the bus driver to get you to school each day. Who else do you rely on? Start with "I rely on . . ." **1**

Now You Try It!

Try defining the next word. Then look up the word in the glossary. Your definition might be better!

com·mun·i·ty

Start with "A *community* is a . . ."**2**
Let's find the word on page 96.

be·long·ings

Start with "*Belongings* are . . ."**3**
Let's find the word on page 95.

★ = New

50

USING VOCABULARY

❶ **Apply:** Using Vocabulary—rely (I rely on my dad to take me to school.)

❷ **Understand:** Defining and Using Vocabulary—community; Using Glossary (A community is a group of people or animals that live and work together.)

❸ **Understand:** Defining and Using Vocabulary—belongings; Using Glossary (Belongings are things that you own.)

CHAPTER 10 INSTRUCTIONS
Students read Chapter 10 with the teacher.

COMPREHENSION PROCESSES
Remember, Understand, Apply, Analyze

PROCEDURES

1. Reviewing Chapter 9

Summarizing; Inferring
Have students turn to page 46. Quickly discuss the questions from Chapter 9, Setting a Purpose. Say something like:
Yesterday, you read Chapter 9 on your own. Let's see what you found out. What happened on January 6? (There was a big snowstorm.)
How did Betsy's family keep the chickens safe?
(They brought the chickens into the dugout.)
What was the family worried about from January 7 to January 12?
(They were worried about Papa. They were worried that he had gotten caught in the snowstorm. They were worried he wouldn't come back.)
What did the family have to be thankful for? (The dugout kept them warm during the winter storm. They had milk to drink and plenty of potatoes and bacon. Papa came back. He was safe. Papa got a surprise for Mama—a piano.)

2. Introducing Chapter 10

Identifying—Title; Inferring
Read and discuss the title. Say something like:
What's the title of this chapter? (Children in the 1800s: Photo Essay)
A photo essay is a story that is told through photographs. Who do you think the photo story is going to be about? (It will be about children in the 1800s.)
This chapter will be a lot of fun. We will get to see photos of real people from the 1800s.

3. First Reading
- Ask questions and discuss the story as indicated by the embedded questions and gray text.
- Mix group and individual turns, independent of your voice.
  Have students work toward a group accuracy goal of 0–6 errors.
- After reading the story, practice any difficult words.
  Reread the story if students have not reached the accuracy goal.

4. Partner or Whisper Reading: Repeated Reading

Before beginning independent work, have students finger track and partner or whisper read.

5. Comprehension and Skill Work
Tell students they will do a Written Assessment after they read Chapter 10. For teacher directions, see pages 108–110.

6. Homework 6: Repeated Reading

WITH THE TEACHER

Chapter 10

Children in the 1800s: Photo Essay

What was life like for children in the West in the 1800s? Thanks to photography, we can see how they lived, worked, and played. Look at the following pictures to see how their lives were different from yours. In what ways were their lives the same as yours?

Photographer taking picture—early 1900s

51

FOCUS ON COMPREHENSION BUILDING

Describing, Making Connections, Comparing

After students read the first sentence in the paragraph, say something like:
Let's talk about that. What was life like for children in the 1800s?
(It was hard. It was full of adventure. Kids had to work, but they were proud of themselves . . .)

After students read the last sentence in the paragraph, say something like:
Let's think about that question. In what ways were the lives of kids in the 1800s the same as yours?
(The kids had chores. They kept in touch with families. They moved . . .)

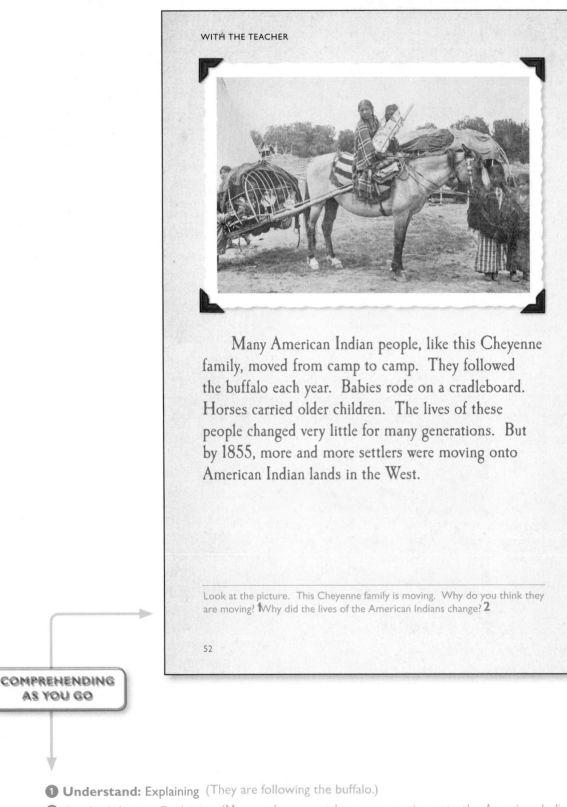

WITH THE TEACHER

Many American Indian people, like this Cheyenne family, moved from camp to camp. They followed the buffalo each year. Babies rode on a cradleboard. Horses carried older children. The lives of these people changed very little for many generations. But by 1855, more and more settlers were moving onto American Indian lands in the West.

Look at the picture. This Cheyenne family is moving. Why do you think they are moving? **1** Why did the lives of the American Indians change? **2**

52

COMPREHENDING
AS YOU GO

1 **Understand:** Explaining (They are following the buffalo.)

2 **Apply:** Inferring, Explaining (More and more settlers were moving onto the American Indian lands in the West.)

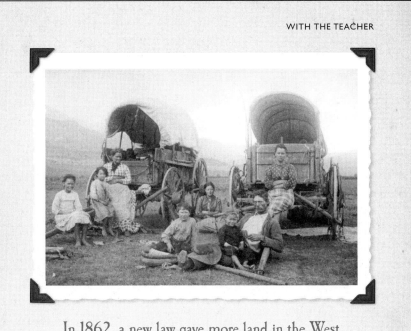

WITH THE TEACHER

In 1862, a new law gave more land in the West to settlers. They could have land if they lived on it for five years. Many pioneer families went west in covered wagons. The wagons carried all of their belongings across prairies and mountains. Once pioneers reached their new land, they often lived in their wagons until they could build a house.

How did *pioneer* families travel to the West?[1] Once they got to the West, what did they do?[2]

53

COMPREHENDING
AS YOU GO

❶ **Understand:** Explaining; Using Vocabulary—pioneer, the West (Pioneer families traveled to the West in covered wagons.)
❷ **Understand:** Explaining (They lived in their wagons until they could build a house.)

WITH THE TEACHER

After 1865, many pioneers set up homesteads in the West. Living on a homestead was hard work. Families had to build houses, plant crops, and raise animals. They often lived far from towns or other houses. They had to rely on themselves. Small children fed chickens and gathered firewood. Older children milked cows, washed clothes, and even hunted.

Describe life on a *homestead*.**1** How was it different from your life?**2**

54

COMPREHENDING
AS YOU GO

1 **Understand:** Describing; Summarizing; Using Vocabulary—homestead (Life on a homestead was hard work. People had to build their own houses, plant crops, and raise animals. Even children had to work. They had to feed chickens, gather firewood, milk cows, and hunt for food.)

2 **Analyze:** Contrasting; **Understand:** Using Vocabulary—pioneer (Pioneer children had to work. They had to feed the chickens and gather firewood. They often lived a long ways from other people. They didn't have TVs, computers, electricity . . .)

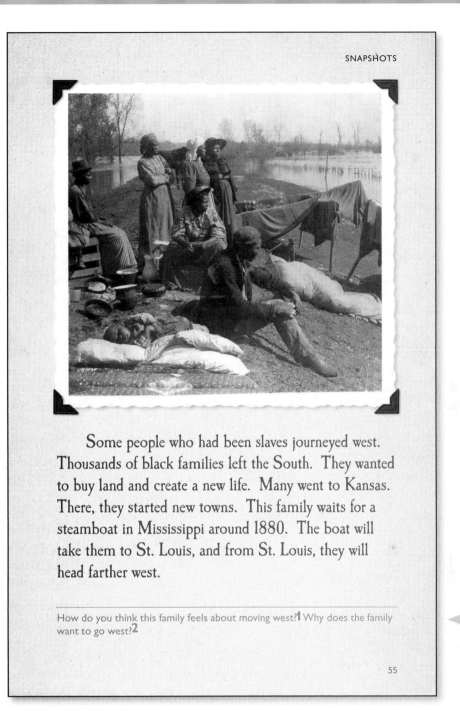

SNAPSHOTS

Some people who had been slaves journeyed west. Thousands of black families left the South. They wanted to buy land and create a new life. Many went to Kansas. There, they started new towns. This family waits for a steamboat in Mississippi around 1880. The boat will take them to St. Louis, and from St. Louis, they will head farther west.

How do you think this family feels about moving west?**1** Why does the family want to go west?**2**

55

COMPREHENDING
AS YOU GO

❶ **Apply:** Inferring, Explaining (They are probably excited to start a new life. They might be a little scared too.)

❷ **Apply:** Inferring, Explaining (They want to move where they can buy land and start a new life.)

WITH THE TEACHER

By 1890, most American Indian families had been forced to live on reservations, land set aside for Indian use. Cheyenne families like this one were moved to reservations in Oklahoma and Montana. These people were no longer allowed to follow the buffalo. The tepee and strips of meat drying outdoors shown here were traditional customs. This family also used tin plates and buckets like the pioneers. Even though they had to get used to new ways, they worked hard to keep their traditions.

How did life in the West change for people like this *Cheyenne* family?**1**

56

COMPREHENDING
AS YOU GO

❶ **Analyze:** Distinguishing Cause/Effect; **Understand:** Using Vocabulary—Cheyenne, reservation
(The Cheyenne people were moved to the reservations. They could no longer follow and hunt the buffalo as they had for hundreds of years.)

SNAPSHOTS

By 1900, more towns were growing in the West. Many families did well in their new towns. They created new communities. Children could go to school. They could play with friends who lived nearby. In small towns in Kansas, children from many places went to school together.

Life was an adventure for children in the West in the 1800s, whatever their background.

What was life like in the West for some pioneer families? **1**

57

COMPREHENDING
AS YOU GO

1 **Understand:** Explaining; Summarizing; Using Vocabulary—pioneer, the West (Some pioneer families moved to new towns in the West. The children went to school and played with friends nearby. It was a good new life . . . By 1900, life looked more like it does today.)

7. **Introducing the Timeline**

   Using Graphic Organizer—Sequence

   Say something like:

   This timeline shows you how some of the events we read about—both real and historical fiction—communicate what life was like in the 1800s.

8. **Reviewing the History of American Indians of the Great Plains During the 1800s**

   Reviewing; Using Graphic Organizer—Sequence; Viewing; Summarizing—Facts

   Say something like:

   The first story we read was "Buffalo Hunt." Touch the picture that shows when this story took place. What year was that? (1835)

   Now look at the photo of the Cheyenne Family. When was that picture taken? (1855)

   From "Buffalo Hunt" and the photo of the Cheyenne family, we learned a little about how the American Indians had lived for hundreds of years.

   What do you know now about American Indians who hunted buffalo? (They had special names that told about them—like Many Falls and Swift Arrow. They followed the buffalo. They used every part of the buffalo for something . . .)

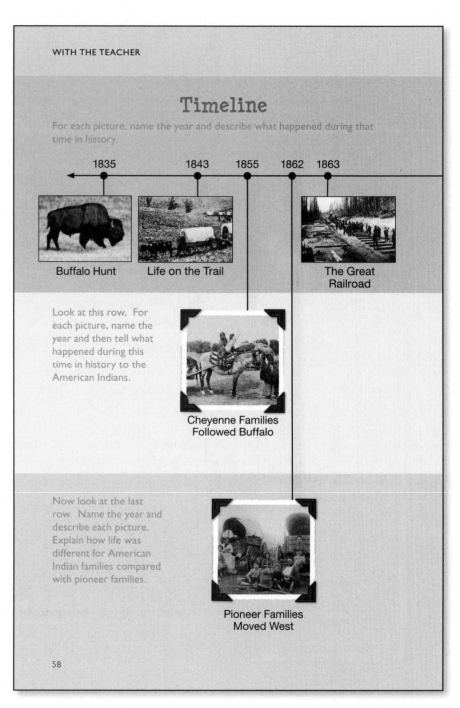

WITH THE TEACHER

Timeline

For each picture, name the year and describe what happened during that time in history.

1835   1843   1855   1862   1863

Buffalo Hunt   Life on the Trail   The Great Railroad

Look at this row. For each picture, name the year and then tell what happened during this time in history to the American Indians.

Cheyenne Families Followed Buffalo

Now look at the last row. Name the year and describe each picture. Explain how life was different for American Indian families compared with pioneer families.

Pioneer Families Moved West

58

Now touch the photo of the American Indian family from 1890.
What happened to that family? (They could no longer hunt buffalo. They were moved to reservations.)

The stories and photos show how life changed in a very big way for American Indians in the 1800s.

9. Reviewing the History of Pioneers in the 1800s

Reviewing; Using Graphic Organizer—Sequence; Viewing; Summarizing—Facts; Using Vocabulary—dawdle

Now touch the picture of the family moving west. How did the early pioneers get to their new homes in the West? (by wagon train) What else did you learn about wagon trains? (The people on the wagon trains had to work hard. Some lost their wagons on the way. Riding in a wagon train was bumpy. They couldn't dawdle . . .)

Look at the timeline again. What important event happened in 1863? (The great railroad was built.)

How did people travel west after the railroad was built? (by train) Yes, and some people went west by steamboat. Find the African American family. When did they head west? (1880)

Finally, look at the photo of 1900. What had happened to America by 1900? That's a little more than 100 years ago. (People built towns and schools out west.)

I am very impressed with what you know about American history. When you take your timelines home, your parents will be very proud of what you can tell them. You are historians. I hope you will read more about the 1800s. There are a lot of interesting stories about the Gold Rush, famous American Indians, and pioneer life.

SNAPSHOTS

1865   1880   1885   1890   1900

Betsy's New Home

American Indians Were Moved to Reservations

Pioneers Made Homes

Black Families Journeyed West

Pioneers Built Schools and Towns

READING BROADLY

For students who enjoyed the historical fiction, you may wish to direct them to the Little House on the Prairie series. Encourage students who enjoyed the nonfiction stories to find other books about this time period at the library.

WRITTEN ASSESSMENT (1 of 3)

COMPREHENSION PROCESSES
Remember, Understand, Apply, Analyze, Evaluate, Create

WRITING TRAITS
**Conventions—Complete Sentence, Capital, Period
Presentation**

Test Taking

Unit 15 Written Assessment
Use after Exercise 6 and Snapshots, Chapter 10

WARM-UP

stagecoach	Missouri	Charlie	invented	machines

The Pony Express

People who went West in the 1800s needed ways to stay in touch with their families in the East. There were no cars or planes. There were no phones. Mail was sent by stagecoach or boat. It could take six months for mail to get from coast to coast. Often it was lost along the way.

In 1860, the Pony Express was started. Young men carried the mail on horses. They rode fast. It took just ten days to get mail from Missouri to the West Coast. Every ten miles, riders would stop and get a fresh horse. Every hundred miles, the riders would pass the mail to the next rider. This way, the men and horses would have time to rest. One of the youngest riders was a boy named Charlie. He was only eleven years old!

The Pony Express worked well. But it lasted for only about a year and a half. What happened? New machines were invented. News could travel from coast to coast in minutes. The Pony Express was no longer needed.

continued

WRITTEN ASSESSMENT (2 of 3)

Identifying—Topic
Sentence Completion

Identifying—Goal; Using Vocabulary—
communicate, the West

Using Graphic Organizer
(Hierarchy Chart); Identifying—
Supporting Details
Using Vocabulary—Missouri

Using Graphic Organizer (Hierarchy
Chart); Inferring—Main Idea
Using Vocabulary—communicate

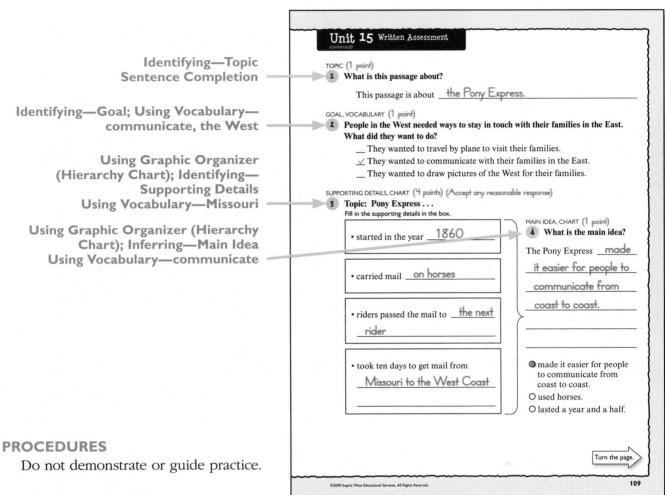

Unit 15 Written Assessment
(continued)

TOPIC (1 point)
1. **What is this passage about?**

This passage is about __the Pony Express.__

GOAL, VOCABULARY (1 point)
2. **People in the West needed ways to stay in touch with their families in the East. What did they want to do?**
   __ They wanted to travel by plane to visit their families.
   _✓_ They wanted to communicate with their families in the East.
   __ They wanted to draw pictures of the West for their families.

SUPPORTING DETAILS, CHART (4 points) (Accept any reasonable response)
3. **Topic: Pony Express . . .**
Fill in the supporting details in the box.

- started in the year __1860__
- carried mail __on horses__
- riders passed the mail to __the next rider__
- took ten days to get mail from __Missouri to the West Coast__

MAIN IDEA, CHART (1 point)
4. **What is the main idea?**

The Pony Express __made it easier for people to communicate from coast to coast.__

- ● made it easier for people to communicate from coast to coast.
- ○ used horses.
- ○ lasted a year and a half.

Turn the page.

109

PROCEDURES

Do not demonstrate or guide practice.

Written Assessment—Basic Instructions

1. Introduce the Written Assessment.
   - Tell students that their work today is an opportunity for them to show what they can do independently. Say something like:

     You should be very proud of your accomplishments. Remember, on a Written Assessment, you get to show me what you can do all by yourself.

   - Tell students they will whisper read the passage and then answer the questions without help.

2. Check for student understanding.
   Say something like:
   Look at your assessment. What are you going to do first? (write my name)
   What are going to do next? (whisper read the passage)
   What will you do after you read the passage? (answer the questions)

   That's great. Now what will you do if you get to a hard question?
   (reread the question snd try again)
   That's right. What should you do if it's still hard? (reread the passage and try again)
   Very good. And if you still aren't sure, what will you do? (do my best and keep going)

WRITTEN ASSESSMENT (3 of 3)

Drawing Conclusions

Inferring

Responding, Generating Ideas, Sentence Completion, Sentence Writing

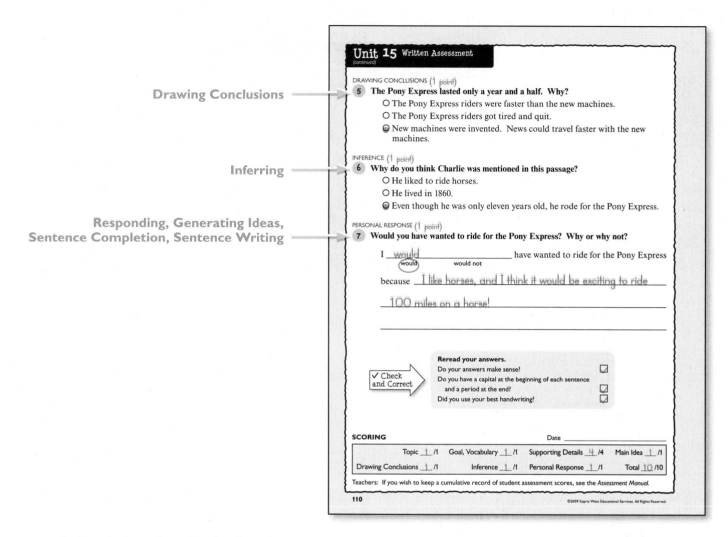

Unit 15 Written Assessment
(continued)

DRAWING CONCLUSIONS (1 point)

5 **The Pony Express lasted only a year and a half. Why?**
- ○ The Pony Express riders were faster than the new machines.
- ○ The Pony Express riders got tired and quit.
- ● New machines were invented. News could travel faster with the new machines.

INFERENCE (1 point)

6 **Why do you think Charlie was mentioned in this passage?**
- ○ He liked to ride horses.
- ○ He lived in 1860.
- ● Even though he was only eleven years old, he rode for the Pony Express.

PERSONAL RESPONSE (1 point)

7 **Would you have wanted to ride for the Pony Express? Why or why not?**

I __would__ have wanted to ride for the Pony Express
(would) / would not

because __I like horses, and I think it would be exciting to ride__

__100 miles on a horse!__

✓ Check and Correct

Reread your answers.
Do your answers make sense? ☑
Do you have a capital at the beginning of each sentence
and a period at the end? ☑
Did you use your best handwriting? ☑

SCORING   Date _____

Topic _1_ /1	Goal, Vocabulary _1_ /1	Supporting Details _4_ /4	Main Idea _1_ /1
Drawing Conclusions _1_ /1	Inference _1_ /1	Personal Response _1_ /1	Total _10_ /10

Teachers: If you wish to keep a cumulative record of student assessment scores, see the *Assessment Manual*.

110   ©2009 Sopris West Educational Services. All Rights Reserved.

3. Remind students to check and correct.

When you finish your assessment, what should you do? (check and correct)

That's right. Go to the top of the page. Reread the questions and make sure your answers make sense. Fix anything that doesn't sound right. Make sure you have an answer for every question.

4. Remind students what to do when they finish their work.

JUST FOR FUN • PACKING THE COVERED WAGON

Unit 15
Use anytime after Chapter 4

Name _____

Just for Fun • Packing the Covered Wagon
What Would You Take?

Pretend you live in America in the 1800s. Your family is moving west. You will be far from friends and family. You have to leave most of your belongings behind. Your clothes have been packed. But you can take one more thing that is very important to you—something that is valuable. What would it be?

1 **Draw a picture of what you would take.**

(Accept any reasonable response.)

2 **Tell what you would take and why.**

My family is moving west in a covered wagon. I can take only one thing besides my clothes. I am taking __a book__

because __then I can read stories at night around the campfire.__

_____

_____

38

©2009 Sopris West Educational Services. All Rights Reserved.

HOW TO USE "JUST FOR FUN" ACTIVITIES

Note: This activity is optional and is *just for fun.* Use the activity:
• as a cushion activity
• for homework
• just for fun

PROCEDURES

Visualizing; Illustrating—Specific Instructions (Item 1)
• Have students read the instructions. Tell them to imagine that their family is loading up a covered wagon to head west. All of their clothes are packed, but there's room for one more belonging. What would they take with them?
• Have students draw a picture of what they would take with them in the covered wagon.

Responding: Sentence Completion—Specific Instructions (Item 2)
Have students complete the sentence telling what they would bring with them on a covered wagon trip.

End of the Unit

In this section, you will find:

Making Decisions

As you near the end of the unit, plan to give the Written Assessment and the Oral Reading Fluency Assessment to each child in your group. Use this section as a general guide for making instructional decisions and doing diagnostic planning.

Written Assessment

The Unit 15 Written Assessment is located on page 107 of *Activity Book 3* and on the CD.

Oral Reading Fluency Assessment

The Unit 15 Oral Reading Fluency Assessment is located on page 116 of this teacher's guide and in the *Assessment Manual*.

Certificate of Achievement

Celebrate your children's accomplishments. When your students master the unit skills, send home the Certificate of Achievement.

Extra Practice Lessons

Use the Extra Practice lessons for students who need additional decoding and fluency work. Student materials can be copied from the Extra Practice blackline masters.

Making Decisions

GENERAL ASSESSMENT GUIDELINES

1. After students read Story Reading 6, "Snapshots of the American West," Chapter 10, give the group the Unit 15 Written Assessment in place of Comprehension and Skill Work. Follow the instructions on pages 108–110 of this guide.

2. While the group is completing the Written Assessment or any time during the day, administer the Oral Reading Fluency Assessment. Assess each student individually.

    Optional: Graph the results of the assessment. (See Unit 7 Teacher's Guide, pages 92 and 95.)
    - If the student's words correct per minute go up, congratulate the student.
    - If the student's words correct per minute go down, discuss the student's overall improvement and help him or her identify ways to improve for the next assessment.

3. Score oral fluency responses on the Student Assessment Record. Adhere to the scoring criteria in the *Assessment Manual*. Use a stopwatch to time how long it takes each student to read the Oral Reading Fluency Passage, and record errors.

USING WRITTEN ASSESSMENT RESULTS

Results of the Written Assessment *should not* be used to determine whether a student or group of students continues forward in the program. As long as students pass the Oral Reading Fluency Assessment, they should continue forward with the next unit.

The Written Assessment should be used to informally monitor how well students read independently and answer questions in writing. If any student has difficulty with the Written Assessment, re-administer the assessment orally.

If the student has difficulty answering the questions orally:
- Record the types of errors (e.g., main idea, sequencing, open-ended response).
- Provide explicit instruction for these types of questions during reading group, before independent work, and in tutorials, as needed.
    1) Demonstrate (or model) appropriate responses, guide practice, and provide opportunities for independent practice.
    2) For inferential questions, think aloud with students—explain how you arrive at an answer.
    3) For literal questions, teach students to reread a passage, locate information, reread the question, and respond.

At the end of each unit, you will need to make decisions regarding student progress. Should students go forward in the program? Does the group need Extra Practice before proceeding? Do individuals require more assistance and practice to continue working in their group? These decisions all require use of the oral reading fluency data and professional judgment. As you analyze assessment results, watch for trends and anomalies.

See the *Assessment Manual* for detailed information and instructional recommendations. General guidelines and recommendations follow:

Strong Pass ≥ 116 WCPM 0–2 errors	• Continue with the current pace of instruction. • Have students set goals. (Until students are reading approximately 180 words correct per minute, oral reading fluency continues to be an instructional goal.)
Pass 95–115 WCPM 0–2 errors	• Continue with the current pace of instruction. Consider increasing fluency practice.
No Pass ≤ 94 WCPM **RED FLAG** A No Pass is a red flag. A mild early intervention can prevent an intense and time-consuming intervention in the future.	• If a child scores a No Pass but has previously passed all assessments, you may wish to advance the student to the next unit, then carefully monitor the student. • If a child scores a No Pass but has previously passed all assessments, you may wish to advance the student to the next unit and also provide additional practice opportunities. (See below.) • If a child scores two consecutive No Passes or periodic No Passes, additional practice must be provided. (See below.) • If a child scores three consecutive No Passes, the student should be placed in a lower-performing group.

Added Practice Options for Groups

Warm-Ups:

• Begin each lesson with Partner Reading of the previous day's homework.

• Begin each day with Partner Reading of a Word Fluency from Extra Practice.

• Begin each lesson with a five-minute Fluency Booster. Place copies of the Unit 7–14 *Read Well* Homework in three-ring notebooks. Each day, have students begin Finger Tracking and Whisper Reading at Unit 7, Homework 1. At the end of five minutes, have students mark where they are in their notebooks. The next day, the goal is to read farther.

• Begin each Story Reading with a review of the previous day's story.

• After reading the story, include Short Passage Practice on a daily basis.

Extended Units: If several children begin to score No Passes or barely pass, extend the unit by adding Extra Practices 1, 2, and/or 3. Extra Practice lessons include Decoding Practice, Fluency Passage, Word Fluency, and a Comprehension and Skill Activity. (See pages 118–124 in this guide.)

Jell-Well Reviews: A Jell-Well Review is the *Read Well* term for a review of earlier units. A Jell-Well Review is a period of time taken to celebrate what children have learned and an opportunity to firm up their foundation of learning. To complete a Jell-Well Review, take the group back to the last unit for which all students scored Strong Passes. Then quickly cycle back up. See the *Assessment Manual* for how to build a Jell-Well Review.

Added Practice Options for Individual Students

Tutorials: Set up five-minute tutorials on a daily basis with an assistant, trained volunteer, or cross-age tutor. Have the tutor provide Short Passage Practice and Timed Readings or Extra Practice lessons.

Double Dose: Find ways to provide a double dose of *Read Well* instruction.
- Have the student work in his or her group *and* a lower-performing group.
- Have an instructional assistant, older student, or parent volunteer preview or review lessons.
- Have an instructional assistant provide instruction with Extra Practice lessons.
- Preview new lessons or review previous lessons.

END-OF-THE-UNIT CELEBRATION

When students pass the Oral Reading Fluency Assessment, celebrate with the Certificate of Achievement on page 117.

Note: Using the Flesch-Kincaid Grade Level readability formula, the Unit 15 Assessment has a 2.8 readability level. Readabilities are based on number of words per sentence and number of syllables per word. Adding one or two multisyllabic words can increase readability by a month or two. Though we are attending to readability for the assessments, the overriding factor is decodability.

TRICKY WORD and FOCUS SKILL WARM-UP

covered	thought	buffalo	Roy	dangerous	traveled

ORAL READING FLUENCY PASSAGE

Imagine the Wild West

⭐Roy enjoyed reading books about the Wild West. He thought it would be fun to live during those times. He thought that being a settler moving to the West would be cool.   9 / 21 / 32

"Riding in a covered wagon would be fun," he told his mother. "I could play in the back of the wagon. I might see buffalo, snakes, and wolves too."   43 / 56 / 61

"It may sound cool, but life was hard," said his mother. "Sometimes the dangerous trip took months. Often, people had to walk behind the wagons. They traveled in the bitter cold and in blazing heat. There were no beds to sleep in, and there were no cars to ride in."   72 / 81 / 93 / 106 / 111

"I think it might be fun for a while but not for a long time," said Roy. "I still like reading about the Wild West, but having a bed and car is a real joy."   125 / 137 / 146

ORAL READING FLUENCY	Start timing at the ⭐. Mark errors. Make a single slash in the text (/) at 60 seconds. If the student completes the passage in less than 60 seconds, have the student go back to the ⭐ and continue reading. Make a double slash (//) in the text at 60 seconds.
WCPM	Determine words correct per minute by subtracting errors from words read in 60 seconds.
STRONG PASS	The student scores no more than 2 errors on the first pass through the passage and reads 116 or more words correct per minute. Proceed to Unit 16.
PASS	The student scores no more than 2 errors on the first pass through the passage and reads 95 to 115 words correct per minute. Proceed to Unit 16.
NO PASS	The student scores 3 or more errors on the first pass through the passage and/or reads 94 or fewer words correct per minute. Provide added fluency practice with *RW2* Unit 15 Extra Practice. (Lessons follow the certificate at the end of the teacher's guide.) After completing the Extra Practice, retest the student.

Hold your head up high!

_____

has successfully completed

Read Well 2 Unit 15 • *Snapshots of the American West*

with _____ words correct per minute.

Teacher Signature _____

Date _____

- - ✂ -

Hold your head up high!

_____

has successfully completed

Read Well 2 Unit 15 • *Snapshots of the American West*

with _____ words correct per minute.

Teacher Signature _____

Date _____

PROCEDURES

1. Sound Review
Use selected Sound Cards from Units 1–15.

2. Sounding Out Smoothly
- For each word, have students say the underlined part, sound out the word smoothly, then read the whole word. Use the words in sentences, as needed.
- Have students read all the words in the row, building accuracy first, then fluency.
- Repeat practice.

3. Accuracy and Fluency Building
- For each task, have students say any underlined part, then read each word.
- Set a pace. Then have students read the whole words in each task and column.
- Repeat practice.

4. Tricky Words
Have students read each row for accuracy, then fluency.

5. Multisyllabic Words
For each word, have students read each syllable out loud, then tell how many syllables are in the word. If needed, use the word in a sentence. Have students read the whole word.

6. Dictation

crawl, hall, hawk, more, store, wore
- Say "crawl." Have students say the word. Guide students as they finger count and say the sounds. Have students touch or write the sounds, then read the word. Say something like:

  The first word is *crawl.* Say the word. (crawl)

  What's the first sound? (/k/) Touch under /k/.
  What's the next sound? (/rrr/) Touch under /rrr/.
  What's the next sound? (/aw/) Write /aw/ with the a-w pattern.
  What's the last sound? (/lll/) Touch under /lll/.
  Read the word. (crawl)

- Repeat with "hall" and "hawk."
- Continue with the rhyming words: more, store, wore.

EXTRA PRACTICE 1

Unit 15 Decoding Practice

Name _____

1. SOUND REVIEW Use selected Sound Cards from Units 1–15.

2. SOUNDING OUT SMOOTHLY Have students say the underlined part, sound out and read each word, then read the row.

hard	herd	new	bow

3. ACCURACY/FLUENCY BUILDING Have students say any underlined part, then read each word. Next, have students read the column.

A1 Buildups	B1 Word Endings	C1 Bossy E	D1 Tricky Words With Endings
joy	knife	snakes	wolf
enjoy	knives	placed	wolf's
enjoyed	dry	fine	wolves
care	dried	tribe	move
scare	thankful	bones	moving
scares	hunter	close	movement
care	killed	whole	have
careful	tattered	used	having
carefully		huge	

4. TRICKY WORDS Have students read each row for accuracy, then fluency.

| A | his | young | wouldn't | enough | friends | 5 |
| B | covered | everyone | months | often | people | 10 |

5. MULTISYLLABIC WORDS Have students read the word by parts, tell how many syllables are in the word, then read the whole word.

A	bow·string	bowstring	mus·cle	muscle
B	ex·pert	expert	ar·row	arrow
C	an·i·mals	animals	buf·fa·lo	buffalo

6. DICTATION Say the word. Have students say the word, then say each sound as they touch or write it.

A1 Shifty Words	B1 Rhyming Words
c r aw l	m o r e
h all	s t o r e
h aw k	w o r e

109

CAUTION
Your children may not need Extra Practice. Use assessment results to determine if Extra Practice is needed.

PROCEDURES

1. First Reading

Mix group and individual turns, independent of your voice. Have students work toward an accuracy goal of 0–2 errors and practice any difficult words.

2. Second Reading, Short Passage Practice: Developing Prosody

- Demonstrate how to read a line or two with expression. Read at a rate slightly faster than the students' rate. Say something like:

  Listen as I read the first two sentences with expression and phrasing. I'm going to emphasize certain words and pause between sentences.

  "Little Hawk was young and small, and he was a great hunter. He crawled on his hands and knees through the tall grass."

- Guide practice with your voice. Now read the paragraph with me.

- Provide individual turns while others track with their fingers and whisper read. Provide descriptive and positive feedback. [Raj], you read with wonderful expression!

EXTRA PRACTICE 1

Unit 15 Fluency Passage

Name _____

Fluency Passage

My goal is to read with 0–2 errors and ____ words correct per minute.

I read with ____ errors and ____ words correct per minute.

The Great Hunter

Little Hawk was young and small, and he was a great hunter. He	13
crawled on his hands and knees through the tall grass. The buffalo	25
herd was just over the hill. Little Hawk wore a wolf's skin so he	39
wouldn't scare the animals. Finally, he was close enough to the huge	51
beasts. He took out his bow and arrow. Then he carefully placed	63
the arrow on the bowstring.	68
Little Hawk let the arrow fly. He was an expert hunter, and he	81
killed the buffalo with one shot. The whole tribe was thankful for	93
his gift. Little Hawk used the buffalo skin to fix a tattered tepee.	106
The men in the tribe used dried muscle to make new bowstrings. His	119
friends made knives from some of the small bones. Everyone in the	131
tribe enjoyed eating the fine meat.	137

Homework
I've listened to my child read this passage twice.   Date _____   Signed _____

©2009 Sopris West Educational Services. All Rights Reserved.

110

3. Partner Reading: Repeated Reading (Checkout Opportunity)

 While students do Partner Reading, listen to individuals read the passage. Work on accuracy and fluency, as needed.

4. Homework: Repeated Reading

 Have students read the story at home.

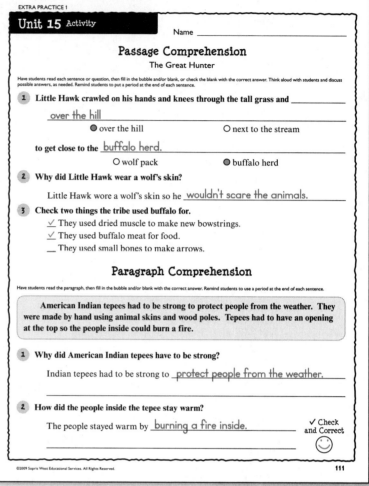

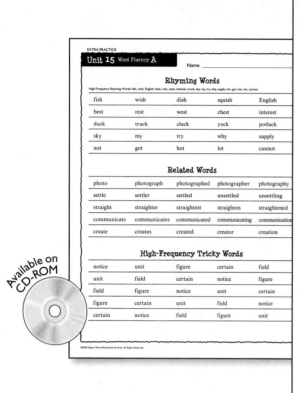

PROCEDURES

For each step, demonstrate and guide practice, as needed. Then have students complete the page independently.

1. Activity
Passage Comprehension
- Have students read each sentence or question, then fill in the bubble and/or blank with the correct answer.
- Think aloud with students and discuss the multiple-choice options, as needed.

Paragraph Comprehension
- Have students read the paragraph.
- Have students read each numbered sentence, then fill in the blank.
- Have students read the completed sentences.

Self-monitoring
Have students read and check their work, then draw a happy face in the Check and Correct circle.

2. Word Fluency (BLMs are located on the CD.)
- To build fluency, have students read Rhyming Words, Related Words, and High-Frequency Tricky Words. Have students read each section three times in a row.
- To build accuracy, have students read all sets with partners.

> **ACCURACY BEFORE FLUENCY**
> **(Reminder)**
> Word Fluency is designed to build accuracy and fluency. Students should practice for accuracy before working on fluency.

PROCEDURES

1. Sound Review

Use selected Sound Cards from Units 1–15.

2. Sounding Out Smoothly

- For each word, have students say the underlined part, sound out the word smoothly, then read the whole word. Use the words in sentences, as needed.
- Have students read all the words in the row, building accuracy first, then fluency.
- Repeat practice.

3. Accuracy and Fluency Building

- For each task, have students say any underlined part, then read each word.
- Set a pace. Then have students read the whole words in each task and column.
- Repeat practice.

4. Tricky Words

Have students read each row for accuracy, then fluency.

5. Multisyllabic Words

For each word, have students read each syllable out loud, then tell how many syllables are in the word. If needed, use the word in a sentence. Have students read the whole word.

6. Dictation

take, took, look, find, mind, behind

- Say "take." Have students say the word. Guide students as they finger count and say the sounds. Have students touch or write the sounds, then read the word.
  The first word is *take.* Say the word. (take)

  What's the first sound? (/t/) Touch under /t/.
  What's the next sound? (/āāā/) Write /āāā/.
  What's the next sound? (/k/) Touch under /k/.
  Read the word. (take)
  Yes, the Bossy E at the end makes letter a say its name.

- Repeat with "took" and "look."
- Continue with the rhyming words: find, mind, behind.

EXTRA PRACTICE 2

Unit 15 Decoding Practice

Name _____

1. SOUND REVIEW Use selected Sound Cards from Units 1–15.

2. SOUNDING OUT SMOOTHLY Have students say the underlined part, sound out and read each word, then read the row.

fence	west	such	milk

3. ACCURACY/FLUENCY BUILDING Have students say any underlined part, then read each word. Next, have students read the column.

A1 Mixed Practice	B1 Word Endings	C1 Rhyming Words	D1 Multisyllabic Words
might	carry	more	Mama
while	carries	chore	Papa
wild		before	Betsy
	dangerous		Willie
plenty	traveled	C2 Bossy E	Irma
ahead		ride	
breakfast	B2 Contractions	riding	D2 Compound Words
settler	can't	blaze	firewood
bitter	it's	blazing	sometimes
gather	he'll	grateful	farmhouse
holler	we'll		

4. TRICKY WORDS Have students read each row for accuracy, then fluency.

| A | early | does | doesn't | busy | wolves | 5 |
| B | says | gone | covered | mother | because | 10 |

5. MULTISYLLABIC WORDS Have students read the word by parts, tell how many syllables are in the word, then read the whole word.

A	be·ing	being	be·hind	behind
B	dur·ing	during	wag·on	wagon
C	buck·ets	buckets	chick·en	chicken

6. DICTATION Say the word. Have students say the word, then say each sound as they touch or write it.

A1 Shifty Words	B1 Rhyming Words
t a k e	f i n d
t o o k	m i n d
l oo k	b e h i n d

112

PROCEDURES

1. First Reading
Have students work toward an accuracy goal of 0–2 errors.

2. Second Reading, Timed Reading: Repeated Reading

- Time individual students for 30 or 60 seconds while the other children track with their fingers and whisper read.
- Determine words correct per minute. Record student scores.

3. Partner Reading: Repeated Reading (Checkout Opportunity)

4. Homework: Repeated Reading

PROCEDURES
Demonstrate and guide practice, as needed.

1. Activity
Passage Comprehension
- Have students read each sentence or question, then check or fill in the blank with the correct answer.
- Think aloud with students and discuss the multiple-choice options, as needed.

Paragraph Comprehension
- Have students read the paragraph.
- Have students read each numbered sentence, then fill in the blank.
- Have students read the completed sentences.

Self-monitoring
Have students read and check their work.

2. Word Fluency (BLMs are located on the CD.)
- To build fluency, have students read Rhyming Words, Related Words, and High-Frequency Tricky Words. Have students read each section three times in a row.
- To build accuracy, have students read all sets with partners.

EXTRA PRACTICE 2

Unit 15 Fluency Passage

Name _____

Fluency Passage

My goal is to read with 0–2 errors and ____ words correct per minute.
I read with ____ errors and ____ words correct per minute.

A Hard Day's Work

Willie and I have a hard day's work ahead of us. Papa took the
covered wagon to town very early this morning. He'll be gone all day.
That means we have to do Papa's chores. Willie says he doesn't mind
doing more work because he has such a fine helper—me!

First, we milk the cows. I stand right behind Willie when he milks
Irma. I don't stand behind Irma because she likes to kick. Willie carries
the buckets of milk into the farmhouse.

Next, I feed the chickens, gather eggs from the hen house, and feed
the pigs. Willie is busy fixing the fence so the wolves can't get into the
hen house.

I hear Mama holler, "Betsy, go get your brother, then come here for
breakfast!" Willie and I still have plenty to do. We'll gather firewood
before lunch. Right now it's time to eat and rest, and I am grateful for
that.

	14
	27
	40
	51
	64
	77
	84
	97
	112
	114
	127
	139
	154
	155

Homework
I've listened to my child read this p...   Signed _____

113

EXTRA PRACTICE 2

Unit 15 Activity

Name _____

Have students read each sentence or question, then fill in or check the blank with the correct answer. Think aloud with students and discuss possible answers, as needed. Remind students to start with a capital and put a period at the end of each sentence.

Passage Comprehension
A Hard Day's Work

1. Check the **two** people who have a **hard** day's work ahead of them.
   — Willie and Papa   ✓ Betsy and Willie
   — Betsy and Mama

2. List two things **Betsy** does while **Willie** is busy fixing the fence.
   • feeds the chickens
   • gathers eggs from the hen house

Have students read the paragraph, then fill in the bubble and/or blank with the correct answer. Remind students to use a capital and a period, as needed.

Paragraph Comprehension

My name is Sam, and it's time for Saturday morning chores. After breakfast, I wash the dirty dishes, clean up my room, and sweep the floors. My brother Dave takes out the trash, cleans up his room, and mows the grass.

1. List two of Sam's chores and two of Da...
   Sam
   • wash the dishes
   • clean up his room

2. (Accept any reasonable response.)
   Who do you think has harder work to do—
   I think Betsy and Willie have h...
   they have to work all day. The...
   carry firewood.

EXTRA PRACTICE

Unit 15 Word Fluency B

Name _____

High-Frequency Rhyming Words: hum, sum, cool, school, am, in, skin, dish, win, begin

Rhyming Words

hum	sum	strum	plum	
cool	school	pool		bubblegum
am	cram	wham	fool	footstool
in	skin	thin	bam	exam
dawn	lawn	prawn	win	begin
		yawn		withdrawn

Related Words

excite	excited	unexcited	exciting	excitement
continue	continued	discontinued	continuing	continuous
luck	lucky	luckier	luckiest	luckily
complete	completed	incomplete	completion	completely
form	reform	inform	former	formerly

High-Frequency Tricky Words

been	toward	walk	want	
toward	want	been	they	
they	walk	toward	been	
walk	they	want	toward	
want	been	they	walk	tow...

PROCEDURES

1. Sound Review
Use selected Sound Cards from Units 1–15.

2. Sounding Out Smoothly
- For each word, have students say the underlined part, sound out the word smoothly, then read the whole word. Use the words in sentences, as needed.
- Have students read all the words in the row, building accuracy first, then fluency.
- Repeat practice.

3. Accuracy and Fluency Building
- For each task, have students say any underlined part, then read each word.
- Set a pace. Then have students read the whole words in each task and column.
- Repeat practice.

4. Tricky Words
Have students read each row for accuracy, then fluency.

5. Multisyllabic Words
For each word, have students read each syllable out loud, then tell how many syllables are in the word. If needed, use the word in a sentence. Have students read the whole word.

6. Dictation

life, light, like, still, stool, stood
- Say "life." Have students say the word. Guide students as they say the sounds. Have students touch or write the sounds, then read the word. Say something like:

The first word is *life.* Say the word. (life)

What's the first sound? (/lll/) Touch under /lll/.
What's the next sound? (/īīī/) Write /īīī/.
What's the last sound? (/fff/) Touch under /fff/.
Read the word. (life)
Yes, the Bossy E at the end makes letter i say its name.

- Repeat with "light" and "like."
- Continue with the shifty words: still, stool, stood.

Unit 15 Decoding Practice

Name _____

1. SOUND REVIEW Use selected Sound Cards from Units 1–15.

2. SOUNDING OUT SMOOTHLY Have students say the underlined part, sound out and read each word, then read the row.

sound	cool	play	back

3. ACCURACY/FLUENCY BUILDING Have students say any underlined part, then read each word. Next, have students read the column.

A1 Sound Practice	B1 Word Endings	C1 Rhyming Words	D1 Tricky Word Buildups
light	sky	gaze	courage
might	skies	graze	discourage
bright	city	amaze	discouraging
told	cities	**C2** Bossy E	**D2** Mixed Practice
cold	cloudy	home	ride
hold	balmy	those	real
Roy	glittering	while	roam
joy	traveled	trade	range
enjoy	dangerous		

4. TRICKY WORDS Have students read each row for accuracy, then fluency.

A	beautiful	beauty	pure	greater	would	5
B	word	often	give	oh	heard	10

5. MULTISYLLABIC WORDS Have students read the word by parts, tell how many syllables are in the word, then read the whole word.

A	set·tler	settler	sel·dom	seldom
B	breez·es	breezes	heav·ens	heavens
C	an·te·lope	antelope	buf·fa·lo	buffalo

6. DICTATION Say the word. Have students say the word, then say each sound as they touch or write it.

A1 Shifty Words	B1 Shifty Words
l i f e	s t i ll
l igh t	s t oo l
l i k e	s t oo d

115

PROCEDURES • FLUENCY PASSAGE

1. First Reading

Have students work toward an accuracy goal of 0–2 errors.

2. Second Reading, Short Passage Practice: Developing Prosody

- Demonstrate how to read a line or two with expression.
- Provide individual turns while others track with their fingers and whisper read.

3. Partner Reading: Repeated Reading (Checkout Opportunity)

While students do Partner Reading, listen to individuals read the passage. Work on accuracy and fluency, as needed.

4. Homework: Repeated Reading

Have students read the passage at home.

PROCEDURES • ACTIVITY, WORD FLUENCY A OR B

1. Activity
Passage Comprehension

- Have students read each sentence or question, then fill in the bubble and/or blank with the correct answer.
- Think aloud with students and discuss the multiple-choice options, as needed.

2. Word Fluency (BLMs are located on the CD.)

You may wish to have students repeat practice with Extra Practice, Word Fluency A or B.

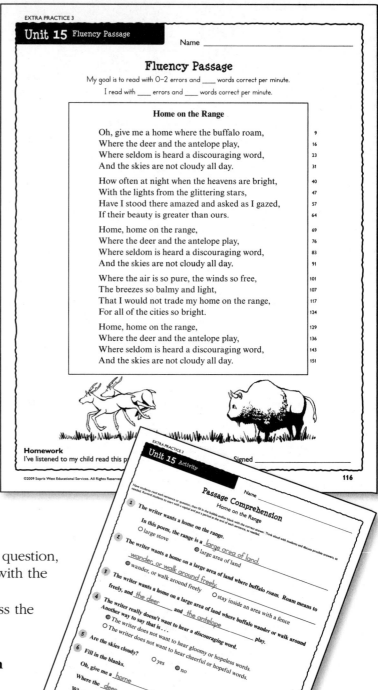